Making Life Work for You

A Training Manual for a Fulfilling Life

Volume 1 in the Successful Living Series

John Schmidt

Path
Publishing

Amarillo, Texas

First edition
Copyright © 2018 John Schmidt

Scriptures marked KJV are taken from the King James Version. Scriptures marked NKJV are taken from *The New King James Bible, New Testament and Psalms.* Nashville: HarperCollins Christian Publishing, 1980.

Path Publishing
4302 SW 51st #121
Amarillo, Texas 79109-6159
USA
Path@PathPublishing.com
PathPublishing.com

To order copies, see About the Author and the Publisher at the end of the book.

ISBN-13: 978-1-891774-25-6
ISBN-10: 1-891774-25-5

Printed in the United States of America

Dedicated to the blessed souls
who never give up.

Determined

It takes some strength to keep on going,
to be aware of a true calling
greater than what normal life might bring.
Let us then put aside
all sadness, and to victory cling,
throwing doors open wide.

(Poetic form: Burns Stanza, a six-line poem
with the rhyme scheme aaabab and
syllable count of 999696)

John Schmidt

Acknowledgments

Mike Bahn, whose business acumen rivals his spiritual
sense and practical giving—a man who I have admired
for many years.

Gary M. Simms, the chess club leader in
"Choices, Chess, and Adolescence"

Ellen Hager, a cousin who kindly sent research
data for "Grandfather's Blessings"

Contents

Introduction

Soon after completing the first draft of this collection of essays, I received a dream which I believe is for the readers of this work and not solely for my understanding. One interpretation leads to this message: We can take the opportunity to examine our lives closely while we still have life, not wait and see what happens after death. But, perhaps you will see more in the dream...

I was shown many brick buildings, unadorned, like old warehouses, side-by-side in a sparsely populated part of a large city. In front of several of the buildings were young men in black suits, unmoving, each posted a few feet away from the front of his building. The buildings were in a U shape around a small square and I could not see their roofs.

At the top of the square was a building with a balding, middle-aged man out front. He was walking near his building when an expensive, black car stopped about 30 feet away. A good-looking, tall young man got out of the back seat and approached the older man, never getting too far away from his car.

"Are you 271?" the young man asked.

The balding man walked backwards two or three steps but was stopped by tall, golden grass about as high as his armpits; the grass looked dead, though there were seeds at the top of the shafts. The balding man raised his right hand to acknowledge that he was 271.

"Can you take me in the building?"

"I have no keys," said the balding man. You have to go get the key and bring it here."

The young man was greatly disappointed.

The balding man said, as if he had been threatened, "What are you going to do to *me*? I have no keys."

I was shown the downtown street nearest the buildings. I could see no cars or people—seemed like the whole downtown area was empty.

The young man turned back to his car, greatly frustrated and pondering what to do.

That was the end of the dream. I got the strong feeling that this is the plight of a human being who is looking for solutions to life after he has died. The tall buildings represent halls of truth, records of the lives of individuals, and more— perhaps the secrets to life itself. Yet these records and secrets are not opened by the young man because it is too late to find out very much after death. Life is not just for the accumulation of goods and services, but for a sincere and persistent investigation into the meaning of life.

Many human beings have had a life cut short, suddenly finding themselves alive yet without a physical body. They remain in their regular world, yet other people suddenly stop talking to them, even stop recognizing their presence. And this can be very frustrating to the newly dead.

People without spiritual education don't even know to call out to Jesus or Father God or an angel for guidance. They never called out when they were alive, so why should they now?

So I ask you, dear reader, to seriously consider the questions and answers in this book. Don't just accept what society has told you is the correct path. Take a long look at life purpose and cause-and-effect reactions while you still have life. Don't wait for the approach of death to force you into a situation of desperate pondering with few clear options as to how to handle the next reality.

Chapter 1

Peaceful Life Purpose

Life purpose is not as mysterious as some people might suppose. If you are looking for your life purpose or want to grow to the next level, whatever you feel that might be, I encourage you to go to a quiet place and ask some of these questions. But ask them not just to your head, but to your heart. Yes, even to your Spirit; though, his response might be very soft, and it might take a while to receive if you have not been listening to him much in the past. I say that not to condemn you, but to free you. We are all on a journey of self-discovery and in the journey there are many doors, pathways, and loving experiences. Love yourself enough to be open to the next experience, the next pathway.

So let's begin, or continue, to ask...

• Where do your talents lie?
• What successes have you had in the past that can be built upon?
• When you dream of being or doing something, what is it that you dream about?
• Who do you admire most? But be careful in this; don't be so enamored with media, entertainment, or sports personalities that you lose sight of someone in your local area who you admire and respect.
• What do you feel most peace about doing? Some teachers and educators say that your desire should require energy and determination. But that might just lead to a whole lot more stress in your life—more stress on your body, your mind, and the people you love most. So get

with yourself in a quiet place and let a feeling of peace be your guide, not anything stressful.

Years ago I wrote this short piece, which I feel is appropriate to insert in this essay. It's title is "To a Young Person Struggling to Find Himself."

When I was a young man, my great desire was to learn more about me and make my mark upon the world. As I did a variety of things, I learned more about me and accepted myself as an okay person. I did not get much attention from other people by my accomplishments, but I learned more about my place in the world. I found that as I accomplished goals I could work long and hard for my approval alone. It was nice when applause came my way, but because I was an okay person I did not need much reminding of my worth. I gradually gravitated toward work that I enjoyed, and that joy increased my sense of worth because I was making at least one person in the world happier: me. I was a bit tense sometimes about following my inner desires, but if I had not, I would never have known the person I am and would have been quite dissatisfied before too long.

As I look back on those years, it seems my greatest errors were in not following inner vision enough—in paying too close attention to advice from other people, especially my peers, and television shows. In those days it would have been hard for me to admit, but my parents were about 90% correct in the advice they gave me, while my peers had a much lower percentage and sometimes got me into trouble. If I had followed most of the advice I found on TV, I would have either gone to jail or gone crazy by the time I was 30. It seems my parents were indeed wiser than my friends or society as it is presented on TV.

Overall, I did pretty well. I learned to listen to the soundness of an argument, even if the words were coming from an adult. I learned to not take advice from a person with little experience in the area of life I might be wondering about. I learned to not take advice about life from a person whose life was a mess. I learned to build a support group of people who had honesty, sound judgement, and a genuine interest in my welfare. Most other people I did not take advice from since I did not know their motives. I made friends slowly, but for life.

Of course I was in a hurry to learn all this and get on with self-sufficiency, but as I look back, I had plenty of time, more than enough time. I had to have time to explore dead-ends; otherwise I would never have known what it was like to be something other than myself. I grew at my own pace; learned to not hurt others; learned to make myself happy, within reason; learned to not conform too much to any society.

And I read somewhere a question that sticks with me even today: When I am dying, what do I want to look back on as having been accomplished in my life? The answer to that question is what a person must be working on.

To conclude this essay, my last word of advice is that at the end of your life, you want to be able to relax with Jesus— both of you smiling in content, looking over a vast ocean of people who have been helped by the work that you, He, the Holy Spirit, Father God, and other people have accomplished.

Chapter 2

God's Kind of Love, Including Forgiveness

People are enamored with the idea of love. They fall in and out of love with people of the opposite sex. They love their cars and new shoes and a multitude of physical objects. They love to go on vacation. So often, the word "love" is a substitute for the word "like" or the phrase "like a whole lot." And I'm not criticizing the use of the word, just saying that let us not forget the most outstanding use of the word. I'm referring to the love of God.

But then again, millions of people have never truly experienced the love of God, so it is easy for them to use the word playfully, in a variety of contexts. Once they experience the love of God, they might use the word more carefully, in far fewer ways.

So how can we experience the love of God? This has been a topic of discussion for theologians for at least 2,000 years. Can I make some suggestions?

First, I believe you have to start thinking of God like a family member. Jesus did. He called Him Father God. And He called the Holy Spirit our Comforter, as one might refer to a good uncle or aunt.

"But the Comforter, which is the Holy Ghost, whom the Father will send in my name, he shall teach you all things, and bring all things to your remembrance, whatsoever I have said unto you" (John 14: 26 KJV).

I know you can't physically see God, but then, there are thousands of things you rely on every day that you cannot see. You have never seen a thought or an emotion, yet you see the results of them constantly. I believe that God is in and around us, doing great work every day; we just don't notice it much. Or we call His activity by other names.

Second, take time to listen. Get out a Bible and start reading, then pause periodically as you would if someone else was in the room, someone who might respond to what you just read or said. Of course, there may be spirits around you who might try to fool you into thinking that they are an audible, or at least a mental, voice from God. If they disturb you, ask Jesus to take them away. Go on reading and enjoy this quiet time. Make Bible reading a habit each day, at least for a few minutes. Once you get in the habit of considering God as someone to listen to, you will receive more good feelings and more insights.

Third, get out in Nature and enjoy the wide variety of His creations. A hundred years ago, when most people worked on farms, this wouldn't be necessary. But we city dwellers, for the most part, could gain physically and spiritually by a good walk in the park or a visit to the country.

Once in Nature, look at or listen to three or four things you never have before. Get down your hands and knees, carefully looking at grass or some other plant, and observe the remarkable variety. This is where a camera might help. Take some pictures and look at them later when you are back home. You will see elements of design that you never noticed before.

Expand your senses. Don't just look at the grass and flowers, but smell them, touch them. Have you ever talked to a flower? I mean, you will not get a response in words, and perhaps in no physical sense at all, but you might get a good feeling from the experience. What is that good feeling all about?

Perhaps that good feeling is associated with the fact that no human being is isolated from other human beings or the planet. We grow up in a social world that is trying to individualize us, help us realize our importance as human beings, but that can go too far. We might be pushed to the point where there *is only* a concern for the individualized self. And that is a shallow and incomplete life. Sometimes we can achieve more in life by letting life itself just fill us, without demands on anything or anyone. That, interestingly enough, might lead you to a fuller experience of God.

Fourth, forgive everybody of everything. God is full of flowing life-energy, and He wants us to flow with Him. Yet we cannot flow if we are building barriers to energy flow. Unforgiveness toward someone is like saying, "I would like to flow and release this person but they did me such harm that I need to insulate myself, build a barrier around some part of me that even God can't touch."

I'm not denying what they did, but that activity, those memories, are in your brain and parts of your physical body. They are always there, day and night, causing your positive energy to go around them, shall we say, in order to properly function. This is not the most efficient use of energy, and it can make you sick.

Try this exercise: Write down the crimes that the other person did to you. Bless the list; ask God to put love energy all around it. Then step back for a second, as if you were somebody else. Ask yourself if this person could really ever pay back the crimes committed? Maybe they are far away, totally out of your life now, and it would be very hard or impossible for them to repay. If repayment is so difficult, why not just let it go, let it pass? Life on Earth is a school. All of us are only students. We all mess up at times, but we can still graduate.

Thurman Scrivner has an outstanding healing ministry called Living Savior. He and Jesus have a very high percentage of breast cancer healings when the women involved are willing to forgive someone. It was Thurman's wife, Cheryl, who deduced that cancer in the left breast was related to the need for forgiveness toward a family member; cancer in the right breast was related to the need for forgiveness toward someone outside the family, or at least the immediate family.

I told an acquaintance of mine about these findings and she was cured; she later said that the chemotherapy was worse on her body than the cancer. Nowadays she has to endure neither one.

The Bible clearly states that we need to forgive others. "Be ye angry, and sin not: let not the sun go down on your wrath" (Ephesians 4:26, KJV).

As someone told me years ago, Father God cannot forgive me of my sins if I don't forgive other people. And I know I have made mistakes, so I certainly want those erased from the Book of Life. As it also says in the Bible, once I forgive, my sins are no longer in God's memory. "I, *even* I, *am* he that blotteth out thy transgressions for mine own sake, and will not remember thy sins" (Isaiah 43:25, KJV).

If He has no remembrance of my mistakes, then why should I? I can then live each day afresh, a new creature in Christ. "Therefore if any man *be* in Christ, *he is* a new creature: old things are passed away; behold, all things are become new" (2 Corinthians 5:17 KJV).

That's what we are talking about here: getting back to God and His simple life for us, enjoying the new strength and wide variety within His love. Imagine yourself walking to a house in the country, opening the door, and seeing an old man seated by the fireplace. He greets you and you smile. Go to him and get a hug. If you have things to let go, talk them out. Repent or cry, whatever you have to do; just get the negative energy out and be at peace.

Chapter 3

Keeping the Peace, in and around Us

To say we all have had disappointments in life is an understatement. We have tons of them: sadness at our parents not living up to our standards when we were children, not being accepted by all of our peers when teenagers, not being able to go to college or technical school, a bad marriage, not getting promoted at work, having health issues, problems with our own children, and the list goes on, unfortunately.

However, there are people who go through life seemingly with very few issues, with a gentle spirit and a smile on their face almost every day. Is there something wrong with these people? As a bumper sticker read: IF YOU'RE NOT DEPRESSED, YOU'RE NOT PAYING ATTENTION. Or, do these delighted individuals have something most people don't perceive or don't live by? Can we take a minute to find out some of their secrets?

Some people are just naturally calm. They are inclined to *not* get upset when something goes wrong. They don't see worry, anger, or retaliation as the solution to any problem. They will put aside their own personal goals and objectives in order to keep peace in the environment. This does not mean they are weak individuals; it just means they have peace and quiet as a high priority. Some observers would say this is a weakness, while others will say this is a strength.

Jesus taught us that calmness is a strength, and yet He would, when appropriate, not back down to vicious authoritarians. Jesus was not a weak person, yet He greatly admired the ability to keep the peace. It appears that His peace came from an inner awareness of the peace of Father God within Him.

What can we learn from these calm individuals? First, that getting upset does not get us to a resolution of an issue. If I drive in my car from Texas heading toward New York City and make a wrong turn, ending up in Wisconsin, it behooves me to get on a right road and not upset my physical body. We can take all kinds of emotional side roads in life, but they usually just make things worse.

Calmness is more efficient. A person can get a whole lot more work done in the day by remaining calm than by getting off on emotional tangents again and again, having to take time to return to stability each time.

And, there is a spiritual force that is enabled when we remain calm. Only in rare cases in the Old Testament do we read where God had to resort to strong measures in dealing with His people. Most of the time calmness reigned. And only twice in the New Testament did Jesus exhibit any form of violence, and that was when He turned over the tables in the Temple. The first time was at the beginning of His ministry and the second time shortly before His crucifixion. He had been for years telling the moneychangers and the Temple authorities to stop taking advantage of the average Jewish believer by charging huge fees for birds to sacrifice, and so forth.

But for those of us who do not have a natural and perhaps ingrained disposition toward calmness, what can we do?

First of all, who is really in charge in this world? If a person believes that God made the world and the universe, and has not abandoned human beings somewhere along the way, then can we not call upon His strength and power when we need to? Some people might say, "I tried that, and nothing happened. I never got my prayers answered."

Allow me to reply with this analogy: If a person has a rich uncle who he never communicated with until there was a crisis somewhere near his 40th birthday, would his uncle be readily inclined to come to his aid? Probably not. Not because the uncle is a bad person, but a strong relationship never was created between the two individuals.

So it can be with a person's relationship with God. If a person "does his own thing" for many years, why should the first prayer, or even the 50th prayer, be answered? Perhaps it is time for the individual to start talking to God as a friend more than a source of benefits. God's unlimited love is always available, so the best time to get started on a relationship is right now.

Second, because human beings have been granted free will by God, some people go far beyond that concept and believe they can do anything to anyone at any time, totally disregarding the laws and principles described in the Bible. Only if they are held in check by the criminal laws in their society do they temper their desires. If we really want peace of mind, and peace in our environments, we need to read the book that tells us how to do that.

Third, a person needs to actively work with the Holy Spirit, Who is a very real part of the Trinity. Issues need to be given to a higher power for true resolution. Then a person can relax and go about his or her daily work without additional stress.

Fourth, sometimes people set themselves up for disappointments by having goals and expectations that are way beyond their ability, and probably not what God intended them to pursue to begin with.

After I had spent more than a decade learning about the writing profession, I talked with a man after church one day who said he was writing his first novel. I remember the delightful spring day as he revealed his plan: he had almost finished writing the book, he would soon send it off to a publisher, and most likely it would be in bookstores that fall, certainly in time for Christmas. Perhaps I was a little too blunt, but I told him he would be very fortunate if the book was in bookstores within two years. Those were the days before the self-publishing revolution, at the start of desktop publishing, and long before print-on-demand printers. A few years later, I learned that he had suffered a nervous breakdown.

Fifth, we need to realize that there is an enemy in the world who is seeking to make our lives as complicated and confusing as possible. Every day we need to seek what the Lord wants us to be doing and say no to unprofitable and stressful goals and ideas.

By aligning ourselves with Christ and the life purpose that God has designed in us, we can greatly reduce the amount of anxiety and stress that we might otherwise have to endure.

Chapter 4

How to Stay Healthy in a Sick World

When I was in my twenties and thirties I lost many relationships because I moved away to take advantage of job opportunities, their mates needed to move far away for some reason, or my wanderlust. Often I moved away from them and then got busy in my new location. There are people who I would like to return to see, but those days are past. They would be too hard to find. The Internet, including Facebook, can be a help, but not always.

As I grow older, I lose people because they go to Heaven. On the fingers of both hands I can count people who had important places in my life and are sometimes very difficult to replace, either with other people or with activities.

I'm tired of this. I'm tired of losing valuable people who had much to give to the world and were cut short in their giving because of health concerns. So I'm writing this essay to ask you to consider lifestyle changes that might literally save your life, allowing you to continue to bring productivity and joy into the lives of other people for as long as possible.

The Bible says we are supposed to live 120 years, minimum. The 70-year time span was related to the Jews in the desert, who denied the importance of taking the Promised Land, as God ordained, and had 50 years cut off the ideal.

Why are so many people not even getting to 70?

What I'm about to tell you may not be popular concepts

or ideas you grew up with, but these health suggestions are widely held by naturopaths, health food store owners and their employees, organic grocers and farmers, and many others. And most of them would agree that the quality of our food has decreased in the last 50 years. So what you grew up with might not work as well as these tips.

Before we get into suggestions, let's talk about money. Does anybody gain money when you are sick? Does anyone gain money by selling you food that is not necessarily healthy for you in the long term—not as healthy as organic food and supplements? Does anyone gain money by getting you addicted to something? I don't just mean liquor and hard drugs—I'm talking about sugar, coffee, food additives, and more.

Where your money goes, your life will follow. You need to understand that there are many people who are willing to let you die in order to make more money. Just think about that. They are not going to warn you about bad habits or how their products lead to bad habits. And the government is in some ways also money driven.

The government is going to warn you about some things, and then ignore other things totally; or the advice they give is going to be so tame that it will allow many evils to come into your diet and your life. The government may not allow into our country much more effective ways of treating some conditions simply because our medical community, as a whole, sometimes makes more money by using archaic and dangerous remedies that often heal only a small percentage of those who are recipients of their prescriptions or violent healing methods.

You must take responsibility. If you want to stay healthy and have a good, long life, only you can take charge. These outside people or forces are often not going to make you savvy and keep you healthy.

On the contrary, there are thousands of people who give good advice. Listen to them. Do not be so afraid of what your family members think or your neighbors think or what relatives think if you need to take more supplements or do other things that will keep you healthy. You are not a child anymore. You are an adult who is responsible for your physical body and your life conditions. Be proactive.

Make a plan to eliminate harmful products and habits, even if you need to gradually work yourself free.

Cut down and gradually eliminate prescription drugs. Usually, a laboratory-produced product can do the one or two things it is designed to do. But so often with our drugs, the effects on the entire body are not examined, not even seriously tested until they are released onto the public. Then if there are serious issues, the FDA will ban the product or demand that marketing containers have more severe warning labels—which most people don't even read, especially if the product was recommended by a doctor—their own doctor or someone on the Internet.

Some people are on several medications, perhaps even a dozen or more. The negative effects of all of the drugs hitting the body at one time (perhaps every day for months or years) can be catastrophic. Sometimes drugs have key ingredients that go by more than one name. The patient has to look at all of the drugs combined and see if every ingredient is going past its limit when other drugs are added into the mix. To make the situation more complicated, an ingredient may go by more than one name or have the same effect as a similar drug or ingredient with an entirely different name. My advice is, slowly cut out the drugs, prescription or street drugs. Seek a naturopath to help you in this process. Keep your life simple and healthy.

Many people believe that organic foods are too expensive. I agree that if you compare an individual item in a health food store to an equivalent grocery store item, you are going to pay more. But not always. Sometimes organic grocers have sale items that are less expensive. Most people don't shop and critically compare prices anyway.

The community in which I live has been blessed with Natural Grocers; I purchase almost all of my groceries from that store. I purchase Gluteno crackers by the case. If your community is not so blessed, go to naturalgrocers.com and do a search on their store location feature. It might be worth even a long drive every few months to be able to purchase items from them. They have been in existence for 60 years.

When the seasons permit, look around for neighborhood or city food markets where individuals gather to sell their produce. But you still must be careful to only purchase from those who promise that they are organic growers.

To be blunt, whom do you want to pay? The organic grocer and his farmers this week or doctors, hospitals, and pharmacists months or years to come? The former path is actually cheaper, certainly when you add in the cost of a funeral and the loss of productivity if a life is shortened 15 to 20 years.

With organic foods you are not going to get the following things:

• Sugar (or at least not much)
• An overabundance of salt
• Food colorings, some of which have names that cannot even be pronounced
• Addictive substances
• Pesticides that are retained in the food because the plants or fruit were sprayed (and the lands that the plants

grew on have been sprayed for years)
• Hormones injected into animals
• Arsenic injected into turkeys to make them fatter around marketing time
• And so much more unwanted stuff

And I do mean "stuff." These really are things you need to avoid. In contrast, with organic foods...

You're going to get simple, nutritious food that your body can actually use without having to eliminate all the unnecessary molecules.

You're going to be able to eat vegetables that have naturally occurring elements that fight off disease. Because the plants were not sprayed with chemicals, they had to fend for themselves against a world of bugs. And this is good. If plants fight bugs, you will end up with far fewer health "bugs" in the long run.

You're going to eat less, most likely, because your body is getting what it needs.

You're going to have far fewer problems with indigestion and stomach issues because your body is not having to do unnecessary work.

You're going to be able to find foods that are gluten free. Look at the word "gluten"; within it you will see the letters that make up the word "glue." That's exactly what gluten does to the digestive track; it sticks like glue to the smaller intestines and makes absorption of the food much harder. Gluten has become a problem because our wheat has deteriorated in quality in the general marketplace.

And certainly, you will not see GMO products on the shelves of organic grocers and health food stores. "Genetically modified" usually means that someone is trying to make the production process cheaper and bypass the rules of Mother Nature. You can think of GMO as standing for...

Goodness
Mostly
Over

Next, let's consider supplements. It's my opinion, and many experts agree, that we cannot get everything our bodies need from food, even organic food. I think it's okay if a person takes 20 or 30 supplements each week. They don't have to be all in the same day. You may take a supplement three times a week, twice a month, or only when you feel a cold might be coming on. But a good multiple vitamin supplement is essential every day. Personally, I also take the following every day:

- Omega 3 fatty acids, even though I eat tuna or salmon with almost every meal
- Vitamins: A, B-Complex, C, D3 (not D or D2), E
- Magnesium

Other helpful products that I take each week, but perhaps not every day:

- Alpha Lipoic Acid (antioxidant and good for the brain)
- Ginkgo (good for the brain)
- CO Q-10 (good for the heart)
- Milk Thistle (good for the liver)
- Calcium

I purchase almost all of my supplements from Puritan Pride, Puritan.com. They have millions of customers.

This is not the complete list, but it will get you started. Incidentally, there is a super product that you need to take when you feel like your body is being attacked and a cold or the flu might come your way. It's called Oscillococcinum. The best price I have found is at Swanson Health Products, which can be easily found on the Internet at SwansonVitamins.com.

Reduce stress. I know you have heard about exercising, getting sufficient sleep, and prayer or meditation. But here are other ideas that might help you.

When I use the word stress, I don't use it in a positive tone. I know some authorities say there is good stress and bad stress. Good stress, I call normal activity, which should in itself have positive stimulants. Yes, one's work is going to have occasional frustrations, but if some of those situations are stressful, they will be overcome. Any activity can sometimes be stressful, even playing with one's children. But that doesn't mean stress must be hung onto and allowed to materialize itself in the body long-term. When I say the word stress, I mean stuff you don't need.

The main thing is to not allow stress in the first place. So often, Americans allow their culture to influence their lives. For example, when people wait in line at a grocery store, why should they get upset? I mean, stuff happens. Let it go. Don't shop at that store anymore. Think about something else. Recite Bible verses to yourself. Talk to somebody else in the line about something positive.

Our society has influences on us in subtle ways also. Like, why does a person need to take on a large mortgage for the next 30 years and have to maintain a house twice the size of his and his family's true needs? The maintenance and all the frustrations that will be coming up could be avoided: lawn mowing twice a month every summer; maintenance on fixtures, appliances, and machines; painting the house every 15 to 20 years; and so much more. A smaller house means less maintenance and less stress.

And think of all the extra money that a person is going to have to come up with when purchasing the home from a bank, thus paying twice to three times its market value. If one has to get a second job, there will be additional stress. If a person cannot find time to talk to his own children because he is always at work, that's more stress. If a husband and wife both work, just barely making ends meet, and then one of them loses their job—well, you get the idea.

Let me tell you my story. When I got out of college I saved enough money to purchase a travel trailer. I saved my money and purchased a mobile home, cash. Heading for retirement, the Holy Spirit encouraged me to sell the mobile home, eliminate maintenance completely, and get an apartment in town. I now live one block from a post office, a barber, a church, and a bank. I no longer have to do very much maintenance on my car since I work at home and drive it so little.

How much money have I paid in interest on housing and cars in my lifetime? *Nothing.* Not one dime. I always paid cash for my cars. The car I currently own has been with me for more than 20 years. But it's very dependable and gets me where I need to go—isn't that the purpose of a car? Why should a car have to be a status symbol or a symbol of personal worth? My worth is in God and His service to people through me.

But living within one's means will take courage. Society says a person should buy a huge house, purchase cars and furniture using loans, perhaps have very little extra cash for fun items, and hopefully get by without a crisis.

I don't like crises. I don't like stress. So I cut down on stress by limiting my goals to things that are reasonable.

One thing about stress and employment: Don't let

ambition hurt your health. As an author, if I don't sell a work or accomplish what I wanted in my writing craft, it's no big deal. God still loves me, and there is always the next book or project I will be doing with Him. Remember, there is no stress in God. So let's live with Him, and in His way of doing things.

One could say that stress is a spiritual issue. If one is not aligned with one's spiritual purpose, there will be duality within the soul. Then the mind will be stressed by the fact that he has to do things he doesn't really want to, because he really and truly wants to follow God's plan. If the mind is stressed, emotions follow. Then emotions influence the physical body and can make it sick. So, find God's plan for your life and don't allow stress to filter down into your body.

Last, let's talk about water. Where does city water come from? Yes, it originally came from rain, a local lake or reservoir, or a river. But after that, where does it come from? Yes, a processing plant near your home, but where do they get most of their water? From the water that you flush down your toilet and water that flows from your bathtub drain and sinks.

I know the city facilities are usually pretty good, sometimes amazingly good at cleaning up water supplies. But what do they have to do to recycle our water? Among other things, they have to use chlorine. If you drank even a small glass of chlorine you would most likely get very ill. And that's only one thing that is added to your water supply.

Millions of people every day purchase bottled water from stores for drinking purposes. And I'm all in favor of that. Even the least expensive bottle of water on a grocery shelf is better than city water. But I would recommend, if at all possible, that you purchase water filters for every faucet or, even better, a reverse-osmosis machine under your kitchen sink. For a few hundred dollars and filter maintenance every year or two, you can have virtually unlimited pure drinking water that you don't have to carry home from a store.

You can also purchase filters that go on your shower nozzle, but I'm not sure you really need to. I don't think city water is greatly absorbed by the body when a person takes a shower. It's much more absorbed when a person takes a bath, but if you feel like you must take a bath and can't do with a shower, then it's better to be clean.

That's it. I could go into greater detail about these things, but this is a game plan for health. If you put these ideas into operation your life will be greatly improved and you will not pass out of the lives of other people nearly as soon. And you will be happier, as you are a greater blessing to the whole world, organic grocers included.

Chapter 5

Choices, Chess, and Adolescence

The teenage years are sometimes the most volatile in one's life. Decisions are made that will affect not only the individual, but parents, siblings, extended family members, peers, a future mate, the community, the country, and the world—the whole range of relationships, I guess one could say.

Why are the teen years often so troublesome? It's not that way in all societies, and not even in the United States 100 to 200 years ago. Can we look at history and find some answers to this question?

Life in the United States 200 years ago was much different. Most people grew up on farms or in small towns that were farm-related, towns that helped farmers do their jobs.

A teenager on a farm was fairly certain to inherit at least a part of the land, be a farmer himself somewhere else, or become a merchant. Yes, there were exceptions. Some left farm life for the big cities where they became employees in factories. Some decided to go west in search of gold, which few of them found. But serious decisions had to be made, and a farm life, though far from secure, was for most boys the best alternative. So they basically did what their parents told them to do.

Girls could rise in society, or at least stabilize their lives, if they were able to marry. If not, they might stay at home and help their parents, or become schoolteachers or nurses, which included being midwives. Their chances for security were even less than the boys'. And there were no backup systems from the government. You either made it or you perished.

Occasional wars did complicate things. It gave the boys a chance to join the military or a marine fleet, once they became of age, but it also greatly increased their chances of being mortality wounded or suffering lifetime handicaps. Wartimes did not help the women either since they could lose potential mates or fathers. And losing a father in those days was a big deal. Not only was the chief breadwinner lost, but the children and the surviving wife were not always able to continue to run the farm as it should be run. As for the mother finding a new mate, that was also a slim chance since most of the men were already married. Men who were not married might be gamblers or thieves. Again, with no government backup systems for the most part, their only hope might be from relatives who could be persuaded to be generous, orphanages, and workhouses—none of which were attractive alternatives.

Educational chances were also vastly limited, especially for individuals who were not with white skin. Even white boys could only be educated if there was a school within walking distance, planting and harvesting did not greatly reduce their time for school, and other obstacles could be overcome. If the man of the house saved enough money for at least one of his boys to go to a two-year college, that was a great achievement. What we call advanced degrees, needless to say, were few and far between. Even most doctors were self-trained. That's why a wife with medical knowledge was so valuable—not only to her family but to neighbors for miles around.

I'm saying all this to paint a picture of an older way of living, where teenagers had far fewer options and therefore could not afford to go through a teenage revolt against their parents, the church, and society in general. Nowadays, even if a teen gets fed up with the home life, he or she can skip out. Life will be very difficult, and I'm not recommending this to anyone, but it happens more frequently in these days.

Yet there are alternatives to leaving home and suffering street-life or minimum-wage jobs for many years. One alternative is to dive into a hobby that will give a new focus, optimism, and the chance to develop skills that can lead to a better way of life once the teen years are finished and difficulties at home are left behind. Sometimes it's hard to convince a teenager that high school and home issues are going to end. But they are.

I need to get personal and relate my own story at this point. When I was about 12 years of age, my parents started on their road toward divorce, which officially occurred in my junior year of high school. That was about five years of confusion and emotional chaos. But I can recall being in an apartment with my mother, with my dad living in the same town in a different apartment, and having a deep sense of serenity come over me. It was as if my own Spirit or some higher being said to me, "It's over." There was no more fighting to listen to, no more chaos.

Once I had fully forgiven my parents, and it took a few years, I was a much better person. Once I forgave them totally, some inner part of me let me see the spiritual workings of our three-person group. I recalled what my mother said one time about a friend of hers in California, in the years when she was dating my dad; the friend had an amazing prediction about his life. The friend said that he would marry three women in his lifetime; the first would be my mother, then a blonde who would pass away, and then a third woman. That was a brave prediction, considering the man was about to marry the first wife. But it turned out to be exactly true.

So putting things together, in the spiritual world and the natural, I deduced that their divorce had been meant to be. That they each had lessons to learn from their relationship and each would go on to other lessons, other mates.

My mother remarried; the man turned out to be an alcoholic, whom she divorced after only a couple years. She once said that one of her brothers was an alcoholic and she could have helped him more, but did not. And after her dad died, she had to help raise several younger brothers and sisters. I have great sympathy for her if she was unable to help the older alcoholic brother, who I believe ran away from home and did not help his younger brothers and sisters. But that was his choice; life on a marginal farm in Central Texas with a group of people to support was not easy to stay with. My mother was born somewhere in the middle of 13 children. But she did learn from those experiences.

I also had to forgive myself. As a young teen, I blamed myself for the divorce of my parents. Looking at it from an adult's point of view, one would think that would be impossible. But many experts say that often happens, the child assumes responsibility for the family breaking up.

I can recall my dad saying at one point, "I wouldn't be here if it wasn't for Johnny." That was a compliment, that he loved me so much that he would stay with a wife who was going through menopause. (That was the diagnosis of a friend of the family who was a nurse; she sympathetically explained to me years later that the medical world did not have much help for any woman going through menopause in those days.) But from my point of view as a child, my thought was, "If I wasn't such a bother, my dad could be free."

Unfortunately, the process of a child coming out of his self-centeredness, in which the individual believes that the entire world revolves around him, takes time to evolve. He eventually realizes that not only is he not the center of family or world happenings, he is also not the cause of family or world problems. He realizes that when his parents have disagreements, those issues for the most part are parental issues and have little to do with him. He is an innocent bystander and needs to bide his time.

For a young person going through a family breakup, I have these suggestions...

Don't join a gang. Don't be influenced by what peers are doing if they are ending up in jail or dead. Find an innocent, creative hobby to get very much involved with and go with it. That's what I did. I joined the chess club at my high school, was introduced to a man who was in charge of the local citywide chess club, and dove into chess playing and chess study. I spent long hours delving into chess books, playing at the club at least once a week, and attending chess tournaments. After a couple years of preparation I found that I did pretty well. That gave me an increased ability to concentrate and confidence, which I greatly needed. Chess playing gave me a chance to be around people who were fun-loving, not at all dangerous, and viewed life as an adventure, one big game.

Yes, schoolwork was important. But the confidence I gained on the chessboard helped me in many ways. Thankfully, my parents always assumed I would go to college. So I went two years to the local junior college and graduated at a university.

It was after the university experience that I stopped playing chess. Not because I didn't enjoy the game, but because I knew God had prepared something new, something wonderful—a career as a writer.

The writing, for the most part, has been a hobby, as chess was in my high school days. But it has given me delightful adventures, chances to help readers all over the world, and even a way to help writers through my own publishing company.

The choices you make in adolescence are very important. Don't spoil your entire life by dwelling on negative experiences. Our society expects teenagers to be like adults when they are too young to get a job and make good money. And that's not fair.

A teenager should have a chance to be what they are, the teenager who is growing into an adult, and not a young adult who is suffering persistent frustration. Life has its stages, and each one is to be enjoyed, lived to its fullest, lived in God's perfect plan for the life. When that happens, we all win. Not only do you win, but your parents go on without guilty feelings about what happened to you, the people you will meet down the road will enjoy your presence because you are much more caring, your future employers will appreciate your positive attitude and your productivity, and society as a whole will gain. You will one day look back on adolescence as an okay time. It had its challenges, but you won the game. You checkmated chaos.

Chapter 6

Grandfather's Blessings

They say generational curses are passed on to unsuspecting souls for perhaps hundreds of years. So are blessings.

Take my grandfather for example. Gottlieb Schmidt arrived on American soil in the early 1900s. My relatives tell me that he was dissatisfied with the German Kaiser. Grandfather was a wise person, and saw that the Kaiser was up to no good.

So, alone, he boarded a ship for a land that held promise, but no great security. He may have had some relatives in North Dakota before he arrived there, but maybe not.

The story has it, from my father, Herman Schmidt, that Grandfather was an excellent tailor. But because he could not speak English very well, the only thing left was farming.

He bought some land with many rocks on it, which he had to move out and place into piles. Personally, I think it was a rough life, at least at first. If you, dear reader, have ever visited North Dakota in the winter, or even in spring or autumn, you can imagine what life was like for him. And in that part of the world, if I'm not mistaken, there are no second planting seasons. Your crops either make it the first time, or you have nothing to sell and not much to eat in the spring. That is why some people call spring the starving season, because if the harvest from the previous year doesn't hold out, there is nothing to eat. Those were the days when there was no government backup, no safety net for anyone except people who were endowed with rich relatives who might help them through tough times.

Anyway, he made it. And amazingly enough, he prospered. When I was in my early teens, my dad and I made a trip from Texas to North Dakota to visit "the farm." I recall the large white house, either two stories with an attic or three stories. I remember that even in the summer it was cold in the house. One of his sons, Fred, lived there with his wife and two boys, the old folks having passed away years before. The old house served very well, until eventually, it burned down, perhaps because of lightning.

Speaking of the old folks, my dad told me this story of how my grandfather found a wife. Women were scarce in that part of the world, especially women who spoke German. So Grandfather ordered a wife through a catalog, which was not an uncommon practice in those days. He paid some money down, and I suppose would have had to pay more upon her arrival and acceptance.

A woman was sent, all the way across the Atlantic Ocean. I'm sure part of Grandfather's fee paid her expenses. She also came alone, and made her way to North Dakota. When she arrived in the small town near his farm, she asked for directions. His farm was within walking distance, so she started out. She came to a farm that she thought might be the right place and knocked on the door.

An older man came to the door, but he did not claim to be my grandfather. They got to talking and he found out that she was soon to be a purchased wife. Well, the story has it that he told her, and I paraphrase, "You don't want to go see old Gottlieb. I have a young son you should marry." And he promptly introduced her to his son, they liked each other, and soon married.

Grandfather wondered why the lady had not shown up, investigated the situation by talking to neighbors, and found out where she had been taken in. He was not a violent person, or even argumentative, so he let it pass. But he did write the company who promised him a wife; they would not return is money, but they did send another woman. I'm not sure if he had to pay additional fees, but he did eventually have on his premises, Marie. They became man and wife.

My dad said that she had a limp, but Gottlieb didn't care. She turned out to be an excellent wife, a hard worker, easy to get along with, and the mother of their four children, one dying in infancy.

So now you know the story, but not all of the story.

As I look back on it, I have much to be thankful for. I come from good stock, hardworking people who had courage, determination, and common sense. They made it in a tough world, far tougher than the times I have endured.

When Gottlieb decided to leave Germany, he influenced not only his own life but generations to come.

If he had not left Germany, he would have been involved in World War I. There was a good chance he would have been drafted as a soldier even if he was middle-aged. The Germans were far more likely to send boys and older men into battle than were the Americans. I have read stories about German boys in battle and their rifles, including bayonets, were taller than they were.

Many people thought in 1920 that World War I would be the last war. How wrong they were. Without grandfather's decision to leave, my father would have grown up as a German and been on the losing side in World War II, with a greater chance of not surviving.

My dad was sent to the Pacific front. I guess in those hard times, Americans with German surnames were sent to fight the Japanese and those with Asian surnames were sent to fight the Germans. That way, nobody could feel like they were shooting their own people. That might have been an important consideration, believe me.

After Dad joined the Coast Guard, he was at one point on a destroyer, which was safer duty than being on a tanker, with German and Japanese submarines sneaking around everywhere.

Dad told me once that if any sailor did not know how to swim, he got a quick training course: He was thrown overboard without a life jacket. I guess they never lost anybody by doing that, but life was tough.

Dad told me about one miracle he went through, though he didn't call it a miracle. When the Americans were fighting the Japanese, island by island, in the effort to get close enough to Japan to mount a land invasion, he was in charge of driving one of the landing crafts. His craft was hit by a Japanese artillery shell. That should have killed at least some of the men. He escaped without a scratch. No one was killed, but the landing craft was in such bad shape that it had to be towed back to the ship.

It wasn't easy, yet Dad survived the war, and he was on the winning side.

As for the next generation, I have grown up in a nation that has not had a war on its own soil. For my entire lifetime, I have never had to go to war.

So Grandfather got all three of us out of great trials by not being on the losing side. If I had grown up in Germany I might not have gone to war, but I would have endured the

Berlin Wall experience and untold hard times.

I give thanks for my grandfather and grandmother, for being guiding lights for my family, including my cousins and their children, who still live in that part of the country. My mom and dad moved back to Texas, where she grew up, so I even escaped North Dakota winters. They met each other during the war, she working in an airplane factory in California and he on leave as a sailor.

Thanks, Grandfather. As you look down from Heaven, your wisdom is continually appreciated.

Chapter 7

Faith, in God, People, or Both?

The old phrase, "keep the faith," is not heard much anymore, or has been exchanged for different words. Or have people truly lost faith in Father God and the values that made our country great? Has faith been replaced for an optimistic practicality, which will be stable as long as there is not a crisis?

When I turn to the dictionary on my computer (Encarta ® World English Dictionary) I find these definitions...

1. belief or trust: belief in, devotion to, or trust in somebody or something, especially without logical proof

2. religion or religious group: a system of religious belief, or the group of people who adhere to it

3. trust in God: belief in and devotion to God

I'm glad that the writer of these definitions has not lost faith in the word "faith," that we still have the word "God" within the definitions, even if many people do not seem to have much faith in God in their daily pursuits.

The purpose of this essay is not to disparage dwindling faith, but to show that we do indeed still have a great deal of faith, to reveal ways we can increase our faith, and to build on the faith we already have in people.

Let's start with the first kind of faith that most of us experienced: faith in our parents. I realize that many readers of this book did not grow up with two parents, or grew up in blended families where they had stepparents. But most people have at least one person who was a faithful caregiver for at least a few years. Those who grew up mostly in orphanages still should be grateful that the founders of that orphanage and employees of that organization provided care as best they could. When I look back on human history, I see many countries where even the idea of an orphanage did not exist. Children were simply left on the streets or at the sides of roads to fend for themselves.

I was fortunate to have two loving parents, who made the development of faith fairly easy. At least one spiritual writer has said that a person's faith in Father God is often founded on the relationship they had with their physical father, his presence and attention. My relationship with my dad was a good one. He faithfully worked at one job for more than 30 years in order to give my mom and me financial stability. Although not an outgoing person, he gave me as much emotional support as other men of his generation, who were taught by their fathers to not show feelings.

As we grow older, we develop faith in our teachers—in schools and churches. Most of what they taught me was reasonable, but to this day I don't understand the necessity for algebra. And I don't understand why God has been removed from most schools, at least the non-Christian schools. But for the most part, these caring individuals have been helpful additions to our lives. They bring a stability to a child's existence over the years, as long as a child stays in school and has parents who will make Sunday School a priority. Unfortunately, millions of parents have lost faith in church education for their children and for themselves.

Children learn to have faith in their country—the ideals,

values, and financial systems that make the country strong. Their faith can be tried when the country's leaders do not live up to those values themselves, but I suppose in every country that ever existed there have been individuals who were mostly out for their own gain despite the fact that they would be poor examples for citizens of all ages.

Still, our leaders must strive to be the very best individuals that they can be, and run the country with honor and idealism.

One of the greatest losses of faith that I see in our country concerns marriage. Many young people have traded the stability of marriage for a temporary "living together." And I can see their point of view, with half the marriages in the nation ending in divorce. But that statistic is most likely caused by a number of factors more than flaws within the institution itself.

The Bible clearly states there is not to be sex outside marriage, calling it "fornication." In my observations over the years, I have noticed that when men have sex outside marriage (adultery included), their bodies become seriously ill. I don't think this is mere coincidence. I think there are fundamental laws about sex and marriage that are not to be broken. I believe that people should remain single, even if they are single throughout their adult lives, rather than suffer physical deterioration long before anyone expected.

We need to maintain faith in the truths stated in the Bible. There is more common sense and spiritual truth in that book than any I know of. Many of the characters in the Bible go through trials, temptations, and calamities—many of them are bad examples, to show us what not to do. But throughout the book there is a thread of morality and loving instruction from God. If we will remain faithful, read the book every day, and apply what we read, we can save a tremendous amount of suffering.

As we progress through the years, we have experiences with people who we can have trust in, and those who prove untrustworthy. Throughout all those experiences, however, we need to maintain a fundamental trust in the goodness of the human soul. I don't mean that all people are actively engaged in spiritual development, but many are. And there is within every human being the potential to become an amazing individual. We must never lose our faith in that possibility, that everyone can be awakened. Some people just take much longer than others.

I wish everyone could have a voluntary and safe near-death experience; I mean, visit Heaven without all the physical trauma that is usually associated with near-death experiences. Imagine for a moment that you are sitting in a chair alone in your bedroom and an angel appears. The angel offers an opportunity for you to see what Heaven is really like, and while there, visit relatives who have gone on before. Would you go, or say you are too busy?

If you really want to grow your faith in a substantial way, be more open to the existence of Heaven. Realize that it is a very real place, just as real as any city or town in your state. Some people make Heaven a day-to-day experience, just as real as the city or town they physically live in.

Other people view Heaven like they consider some little town on the other side of their state. They may have an admiration for the idea of Heaven, as if it were a town they might like to visit someday, but only after they are finished with what they are personally involved with now. I wish we would all make Heaven a day-to-day reality and consequently make radical changes in our physical and emotional lives.

Don't forget to continue to have faith in yourself. No matter who you are, you have gone through many trials and survived them. Pray every day, believing that you and God can do many other things in the future that will increase your character and also improve the lives of other people. Nobody is perfect. We should not expect ourselves to be perfect. We need to allow ourselves time to grow without being too tough on ourselves. God has already been so very patient, and He will continue to be.

That doesn't mean that we can ignore His wishes for us. But if we remain faithful to the purpose that He has placed in us, faith really can see us through—to the end of this life and beyond, to rewards far greater than we have ever imagined.

Chapter 8

Being a Child Again

For many people, childhood was a traumatic experience. Perhaps even in the womb the mother was an indifferent carrier, who didn't consider her diet and her living habits as affecting the child who was to become a living, breathing, walking human being. Then the hospital personnel, though with all good intentions, stuck needles in infant to protect it from the diabolic world of germs. Followed by a long list of early childhood challenges: perhaps insufficient food or not the right food at the right times; parental indifference, or at least long hours in daycare centers because both parents had jobs; sibling rivalry in various forms; perhaps physical, emotional, or verbal abuse; being raised by parents who followed the patterns of their parents without making any a attempt to discover better ways of doing things; and so much more. It's really amazing that most people come out as well as they do.

In contrast, some of us felt the love of the mother even in the womb. Both mother and father worked hard to provide physical needs and emotional comfort. The spiritual aspects of life were not ignored, encouraging the child to pray before bed and memorize Bible verses, putting forth the effort to see to it that the child could attend Sunday School, and discussing with the child what is wrong with evolution and many of the programs on secular TV. Although not perfect in every way, these caring and giving parents raised children who became responsible adults and treated their children in the ways of the righteous, building a stronger nation in the process.

The purpose of this article is to explore many of the positive aspects of the child condition, in its various aspects, so that we might, as adults, not forget what is good and positive, incorporating many of these positive attributes in our adult lives. By exploring a variety of topics, I will necessarily enter the domains of other chapters in this book; but I don't think merely touching on these ideas will greatly duplicate the content in those other chapters.

Quite often, as adults we get settled in our routine: one job, spouse, house, lawn mower, dog, even the streets we drive on going to and from work. But to a child, almost everything is new and different. Even going into a neighbor's backyard can be a way to see something for the first time. And going to an uncle's house for Thanksgiving can be like going into a whole new world. What we adults see as familiar, or at least close to what we saw a year ago at Thanksgiving, is brightly different to a child.

I don't think it would hurt us adults to get out of the routine once in a while, even if only to take a different route coming home from work or visiting a new restaurant or attending a meeting of a club that is based on some interest we have had since childhood. The old saying is, variety is the spice of life, and that most likely has some truth in it.

In this exploring of the new and different, the child is bound to make mistakes. That's why parents try to foresee dangers. Yet we adults should not be traumatized by the thought of making mistakes when we try something new. We don't have to be experts at everything. If we go to an amusement park or play catch with our kids and their friends, we don't have to ride the biggest ride or be perfect in our pitching technique. Being enthusiastic may be just fine.

I think children can give us a whole new perspective on something once in a while. That's why we sometimes laugh at what they say. We don't mean to be unkind, but they can bring a freshness to practically anything. And they are learning the very basics of speech and social expectations, so they are bound to see things differently from someone who has been around at least two decades—i.e., parents.

I think every child should be allowed the freedom to explore sports, arts, and new environments whenever possible. I wish every child could at least visit a school devoted to creative arts. I think in our future schools a hundred years from now, book learning and memorization will be secondary to creative exploration and the appreciation of animals, plants, and rocks. An ideal school would allow a child to develop in a variety of ways, not having to take tests (which are often very subjective and psychologically damaging to a child) in order to learn. Whether we realize it or not, a child is geared for learning. If that learning is not shut down by rigid school regulations (though of course, order must be maintained—I'm not talking about allowing chaos), then learning can expand in a variety of delightful and perhaps astounding ways.

For a fuller description of what our future educational systems can be like, read one or both of my books about the future, *My Visit to the Kingdom of God* and *My Return to the Future, 2350*, listed at the back of this book in the About the Author and the Publisher section.

Children are remarkably resilient. They can be bored one minute, yet highly involved in something three minutes later. And that something could be as simple as a spider on a wall. I think when we have to punish a child for misbehavior, we don't need to feel guilty about it. If we can hug the child later and let him know that he is still very much loved, he will bounce back.

I wish parents would hug and touch their children often. American society has an odd notion that any touching may surely have sexual connotations. This is so strange. For thousands of years human beings have been close to each other, grooming each other, hugging each other, and not having to analyze their behavior like some sad psychiatrist closely observing his patient for character flaws. I realize that in the workplace we have to be more careful, and not approach others in sexual ways, but we need to, whenever possible, offer a pat on the back when a job has been well done.

Same with the words said to children: We don't have to worry about praising them too much. In their exploration into a world that is challenging, they already feel insecure about not doing everything as well as their parents or some of their peers. So we should not hold back on compliments when they do something right. Let us dispel forever the odd notion that praise can hurt a child's ego. Just the opposite is true. I don't mean we have to praise the child every six to ten minutes, but mentioning something praiseworthy every day or two would not hurt.

One of the most important aspects of childhood that American society tends to almost totally ignore is a child's ability to remember a spiritual past and accept the reality of life beyond the physical.

We never ask the child what it was like before he was born. I don't mean to get weird or metaphysical here, but the child is a spiritual being with a physical body and the Spirit, who is the real child, had to be somewhere before the birth of the physical body. And often a revelation can come to the understanding of both parent and child if we allow him to appreciate his memories. If we never mention anything prior to birth, then he will dismiss any thoughts in that direction.

If we explain to a child that he is a spirit being who has taken a physical body for a while, then that will in many ways negate a fear of death that he will be introduced to later in life. For most Americans, the prospect of death is not attractive. But if we understand that we came from a heavenly existence and are at death returning to a heavenly system, a lot of the fear about losing the physical body does not have the opportunity to take hold.

We Americans also dismiss our children's comments about invisible playmates. Who is to say these playmates are not real? Again, a child recently came from a spiritual world into a physical world, and perhaps he is able to see more of the spiritual world than adults can.

When anyone dies, does he immediately go to Heaven or does he have the freedom to stay on earth and hang around us physical beings, even though we cannot see him? If that person is a child, he may seek out children about his own age and play with them as he once did with his physical playmates.

My mother is one example of a person who was not accepted for all of her spiritual gifts. As a child, she could see the energy fields around people, which we might call auras. She was ridiculed for trying to explain what she saw, so she shut up and kept it to herself. In all the years that I knew her, she only mentioned this to me one time, but I did not ridicule her and I was sympathetic for what she went through.

I think children are much more receptive to the presence of angels and other higher beings than we adults are. Many adults have been schooled in the belief that angels existed in the Bible days, but they have gone away somewhere and have little or no influence in our lives. Children are often much more able to see higher forms of life and will tell us about them if we will encourage them to do so.

I realize there are demonic forces in the world who might try to fool our children as much as they try to fool us adults in a variety of ways, but we can explain that also to our children as long as we don't make them fearful. If we tell them about Jesus, and His presence with us at all times, that will help the situation.

I don't think it's ever too soon to tell a child about Jesus and ask the child to devote his life to Him. Perhaps the child cannot fully understand spiritual life, but accepting Jesus will set the tone for his life. You, as the parent or guardian, set the tone for the household, and when you dedicate your child to Father God, Jesus, and the Holy Spirit, you have set the child on the right path. And, very importantly, Heaven pays attention and becomes an important guide and protector for the child for all the years to come—especially if the child grows into someone who, with adult understanding, accepts the Holy Trinity as a very real partner in life, wherever life may take him.

We should be open to the idea of allowing children to teach us. So often, it is a one-way street, from parent to child or teacher to child. Yet because a child has so many things to teach us, let's be open to new ways of seeing the world in which we live by allowing our children to be a new set of eyes for us all.

Chapter 9

Tithing, Our Friend

Tithing is one of the most difficult topics for a preacher to talk about. Even if we hear an evangelist on TV talking about the topic, it's really easy to go to the next channel.

One of the exceptions to this situation is a message I recently heard from Andy Stanley, who I highly recommend at all times; if you cannot find his program on your TV listing, go to his website, www.yourmove.is.

Andy was able to make tithing a palpable topic by expanding it into "sharing." And he went on to describe the advantages of sharing as opposed to not sharing.

But why is tithing usually a difficult topic? Let me first tell you my story, how tithing has been a huge blessing in my life.

Years ago, when I was in my twenties, I heard about tithing but did not seriously consider doing it. I was just barely getting by as it was. Over the years, I heard messages on tithing and became softened to the idea gradually. Here is the reasoning that developed...

First of all, where does all the energy on this planet come from? Where did our bodies come from, and all the blessings we have received for many years, especially those childhood years when we could not get jobs to support ourselves? Who generates a miracle when we need one? When we look up at the stars at night, who made them?

Where does the energy come from when we awaken each morning refreshed? Does the energy spontaneously arrive from the trillions of cells in our bodies getting together in a collective voice and saying, "We have had time to rest, so now we feel much better"? Or does the energy truly and more subtly arrive from Father God into and through the cells and back to us on the conscious level?

If we have any desire to repay God for all these blessings, how do we repay? Yes, He desires a relationship with us, and we with Him when we are wise. But on the material plane, perhaps words are not enough. We have received physical goods and services. And according to His Bible, we need to take some kind of action in a financial way.

Yes, we can do good deeds for other people and give them encouraging words. But still, we need to go beyond words, for there continues to be a monetary factor that needs to be acted on.

Thus, giving 10% of our income is a great way to bless all of our money, to give thanks for all that we have. God still allows us to keep 90%. If you ever try to create a star or perform a miracle by your own power, you might consider this a bargain. Many people have started to tithe and found that their 90% went a lot further than 100% in the old days ever did. (Though, it may take a few months for the benefits of tithing to kick in.) We might put it this way: Giving 10% allows the Holy Spirit to take greater interest in our wealth, protecting it and guiding its growth.

Second, how do we accomplish payment once we decide to give tithing a try? I think tithing is such a difficult problem for some pastors because they are asking people to pay 10% before taxes. Let me explain.

Let's say you have photocopy of a dollar bill in front of

49

you. I come along with a knife or a pair scissors and cut off a third or a half of the bill. How much do you have left—70%, 60%, 50%? What if I ask you to pay a tithe on what's left? What does reasoning tell you if I ask you to pay 10% on what you have and what I took? Does my second request seem reasonable, or fair? Maybe not.

It's the same way with taxes. The government takes the following taxes from us: income taxes, Social Security taxes, sales taxes, property taxes, gasoline taxes, and hidden taxes we don't even know about. After the government takes all of its taxes, how much is left—70%, 60%, 50%?

If I were a pastor, I would much rather have half or more of my congregation giving 10% of what they bring in after taxes than 10% to 20% of the people giving a tithe on everything and other people giving occasional or small offerings. I am not saying these are typical statistics in all churches, but that's what I have heard from authorities who should know. So my reasoning may stand the test of time and experience.

Third, I developed a practical system that has worked for me for decades. I'm not rich, but I have not had medical expenses in many years, my machines rarely break (though parts or whole machines eventually wear out, of course), and I have peace of mind.

I do not tithe on medical expenses, my pre-need funeral plan, legal fees, or auto repairs—major expenses that might be sudden and very expensive.

I'm able to give where I am being spiritually fed. I have about 20 churches and charities I give to during the year, and not every year do I give to all 20. As Andy Stanley would say, in this way I have the ability to say no to any organization that falls outside my top 20, and I have no regrets. New opportunities for giving may earn top-20 status as the years progress, but not right now.

I can also go beyond the 10% if I want to give to a charity that feeds children or does some other beneficial care for humanity—that is often called an offering.

Fourth, when we start tithing, Father God can bless us in unexpected ways and take care of us in a variety of circumstances. When I applied for my first really good job, years ago, I told the Lord that if He gave me a position fresh out of graduate school, I would back-tithe. That is, I would total up the amount of money I had earned through all the years before, going back to my first job as a high school student, and pay 10% on all those dollars.

Well, I got a job as a teacher in a year when teachers were very plentiful. In only a year I had done the entire back-tithe. So I could then say that for my entire lifetime I have been a tither.

You don't have to back-tithe. That's just something I felt like I wanted to do. But you can start tithing as soon as possible. If you feel like you can't go 10%, still give something. Tell the Lord that you are just learning about tithing and you want to start somewhere. Then go for it.

Take your tithe check, or whatever you can give as an offering, and hold it in your hands. Bless your gift, and all your money. Visualize your money going out to the church of your choice, children in some far off orphanage, a missionary who has the ability to purchase and hand out tracts that save souls—visualize all kinds of things that your dollars might be accomplishing. Get that good feeling down in your soul, and if you cry in joy, all the better.

Chapter 10

Who Is the Holy Spirit?

For non-Christians, I need to explain that Christians believe that the Godhead is composed of three distinct entities:

Father God, in Whom we move and have our being.

Jesus Christ, the son Who died about 2000 years ago but resurrected and continues to be an active part of our lives.

The Holy Spirit, Who many believe has been active since the beginning of Creation.

The purpose of this essay is to enlarge our view of the Holy Spirit in order that we can make Him a greater part of our lives. The purpose of this essay is not to debate the fine points of doctrine within many denominations. To me, we need to be allowed our different opinions and not turn our backs on the fundamental understanding that the Holy Spirit loves us and also wants to be part of our lives, just as much as Father God and Jesus.

Please allow me to start with a concept that has been around for thousands of years but is not totally understood by most people. When we look at life on Earth, what do we see? We see the mineral world, plants, animals, and human beings. Modern science has taught us that there is a marvelous world within the lives of cells and atoms, which are also visible with instruments.

Beyond physical reality, many people can perceive angels. Thousands of people have described incidents where miracles occurred when they contacted angels. For any skeptical reader, simply do an Internet search under "angels and miracles" or go your public library and you hopefully will find examples.

In the Bible, archangels are also mentioned. I believe they exist, just as angels exist.

So how many planes of life do we have? Not counting the atoms and cells, which are a whole different plane of life in themselves, yet counting angels and archangels, there are six. Since the Bible has many examples of the number seven as being the number of completion, can we not include an even higher level of angelic life which I call super angels? That would complete seven levels of conscious life on this planet.

The next question to ask is, are the angels interested in helping humans get through life? I think the answer is obvious: They do. And I think a great deal of their effort is totally unseen and unrecognized by the vast majority of human beings. But that does not change their reality or their efforts. It just makes the recipients appreciative, yet still perhaps totally unaware. Though, in all fairness, humans are gradually waking up to the reality of angelic forces and miracles.

Allow me to go on to the next idea: That many human beings who have passed on into the other world at death and go to Heaven are not content to stay there. Yes, Heaven is a wonderful place to be, but I believe that many human beings continue to have a strong desire to help humanity through this difficult transition from an old world of chaos into the Kingdom of God. Therefore, Father God allows them to return to help if they wish. They no longer have physical bodies, but they do have minds and spirits. Thus, they can do very much to help influence human beings in positive ways.

Your challenge as a physical human being is to learn to distinguish between the voices of these bodiless human beings who want to help you and Satan's forces, who want to destroy you. I will give you a hint: Stay in the Word of God day and night for the rest of your life. The creative forces will be attracted to your thoughts and words since they relate to the Word of God. Simultaneously, Satan's forces will be repulsed.

I think the Holy Spirit has been underrated, shall we say, by many people for a very long time. But if we were to say that the Holy Spirit contains the angels and returning human beings, then we take a great step toward making the Holy Spirit a much greater reality in our lives.

And why shouldn't we allow this to happen? Is it not better to pray for a very real Holy Spirit to be part of our lives, one Who is in part, Michael the archangel? Personally, I want all the help I can get. And in this way, we have a very real Holy Spirit to talk to and pray with. I hope you will join me—I mean, us.

Chapter 11

Angels Everywhere

Most people do not make angels a serious part of their lives. When they do see someone who takes angels seriously, they may think that person is a New Age follower or a little odd. And I don't totally deny the validity of those opinions. But is that the fault of the angels themselves?

The Bible says that angels are messengers who communicate between God and human beings. I think that is definitely one function, but I believe they have a much wider influence on us than we imagine, as a city has more businesses within its boundaries than the various communications services.

And I believe angels have functions in the continuance and organization of this planet that human beings rarely consider. The purpose of this essay is not to convince you to purchase angel jewelry, but to give proper appreciation for beings who love us very much and serve us with very little appreciation.

I'm not saying that all of the manifestations of the miraculous discussed in this essay are caused solely by angels. There may be other causes for the same incidents. Like, if a young person is confronted with a situation where an adult is trapped under a car, and that young person is somehow able to lift the vehicle so the adult can escape, perhaps the strength did not come from an angel. But then, there has to be some cause, and I don't think adrenaline alone could do the job.

Miracles happen in this country every day and they are not reported by the news media. In fact, the news media has a rather low opinion of anything miraculous or spiritual. If a criminal does something irrational and hurts many people, he has far greater chances of making the news programs than the angel who stood between him and others who might have been hurt. The man can be seen on the physical plane but the angel cannot, and that makes all the difference to many people.

I think when Christians call out to Jesus or Father God for assistance, often it is an angel who shows up. To me, angels are members of the Holy Spirit; therefore, we are truly receiving attention from a part of the Godhead when in the presence of an angel. I make no fine distinctions. Help is help, however Heaven wishes to proceed.

Let me also expand the definition of "angel." I believe that many human beings, once they pass on and find themselves in Heaven, hear the cries of those below and return to aid us in any way they can. Some authorities call these entities, "common angels." That's as good a name as any, I suppose. Though, human-angels might be more appropriate; yet that term might be confusing to some people. Whatever we call them, they do indeed exist, in great abundance throughout the world.

The Bible speaks of the "Spiritual Gift of Discernment," one of the nine gifts from the Holy Spirit when a person is receptive. "To another the working of miracles; to another prophecy; to another discerning of spirits; to another *divers* kinds of tongues; to another the interpretation of tongues" (1 Corinthians 12:10, KJV). The gift does not apply only to an awareness of negative influences, but includes the great numbers of heavenly entities who inhabit this planet. Human beings are no more isolated when it comes to spiritual abilities than children playing in one city park are totally removed from the entire population of the city. Our unawareness does not make the variety of spiritual beings cease to exist.

When a person escapes day-to-day life by walking into a country scene or a city park, why is there often an exhilaration that is not easily explained? Could it be the influence of angels or the atmosphere they left behind?

Furthermore, could the extraordinary variety of plant life and animal life on Earth be related to angelic activity? I realize that DNA plays a factor in every birth of everything. But can DNA by itself produce beauty? How could it, if it is unable to see beyond its own complex world? Do we not have to have an entity outside an object of beauty to appreciate the beauty? Additionally, how could DNA by itself coordinate symbiotic relationships or the perfect harmony that exists when various animals feed on plant life within a given area without competing with each other? Therefore, my conclusion is that angels and higher beings are continually active in producing the variety of life forms on Earth.

I contend that angels also help maintain the planet's precise revolution through space, especially after atomic bombs are released by human beings.

Angelic forces help balance atmospheric conditions when the mental lives of the human beings moving around on this planet could make things a whole lot worse than they already are. In the Bible there are cases where a nation turned against God and suffered calamity, total physical destruction or slavery for hundreds of years. Why do we believe that our thoughts and actions have no or little influence on weather patterns? Of course, many of the same people believe that their thoughts do not really influence their own lives, that they can get whatever they want and do whatever they want while thinking whatever they want to think—as if the law of cause and effect applies to everything in the universe *except* human beings.

I believe even before human beings are born, angels are aware. I believe they help human Spirits, who are about to take on physical bodies, to decide what lives to live and choose the parents they need. Angels help design a lifetime of fullness, exploring opportunities for character growth, yet not making a lifetime simply too much to endure. That projection into the future is a fine art. Designing the life of one person requires an understanding of the culture a person will be born into and future world events. Angelic perception can be invaluable because angels see far beyond our three-dimensional world. So I am thankful that our lifetimes, including our life purposes, are not left to human Spirits alone.

And once a person passes away into the next world, I think an angel is there to lead them into that world. If a person has denied God and has been really rotten to people in general, then a trip to Hell is inevitable, and no angel can fix that. Though angels are constantly trying to influence human beings to repent of their sins before the hour of death. Most people do not understand that their sins are not held against them until they lose the physical body; they can repent even in the last minute of life. But that's cutting it awfully close.

An angel has the ability to look at a deceased soul and create a visual image in space that represents all the parts of the life just lived. Additionally, within each representation of a part of the life, there is a sense of the good that was done or the harm—and the lesson that could have been learned or was learned. That is an amazing complexity that surpasses any painting any human being has ever created. From that image, the human can then fully understand the importance the life and what could have been done. The human also takes away from the image an understanding of all the good and bad that was done in the lifetime. It's like a life summary, a final exam, that is given in pure love without any incrimination. This doesn't happen for all people when they pass away. But when it does, there is much greater understanding of the experience we call life and the God Who has mercifully given us the chance to do very well.

And it is an angel, or some higher being, who records the life in heavenly records. Everyone is there, whether they lived their lives appropriately or wish they had done much better.

When a person passes away, his or her guardian angel goes off duty, I suppose we could say. I do not believe that the concept of a guardian angel is simply an old tale. I think many mothers down through the generations have sensed or seen an angel hovering above their child as it slept during a dark night. And how many guardian angels have tears in their eyes when their people mess up real bad, commit suicide, or live immoral lives for decades and die without repentance, without a reunification of their relationship with their God? That reunion could have been accomplished in any minute during the entire lifetime by simply saying, "Jesus, forgive me, come into my heart, and make me a new person. I forgive everyone and myself if You will forgive me." And He wants to forgive them.

That one sentence, and the sincerity behind it, is the difference between eternity in peace or torment.

When I get to Heaven I'm going to walk and talk with more angels than I have ever had the pleasure of meeting. We get so caught up in our physical lives—the ambitions, needs, wants, people—all of it. If we would only take the time to allow angels to play a larger part in our lives now, we would indeed be happier. But there, in Heaven, we will have the opportunity to walk and speak with those who we never knew existed. And even beyond this world, we will be with them to explore new worlds, new solar systems, new galaxies. To get there, isn't doing well in this life worth the effort?

Chapter 12

Helping Suicide Prevention Helpers

Most human beings have contemplated suicide at one time or another. Luckily, the vast majority of those individuals did not do it. They went on to live fulfilled lives, their closest relatives were spared great sadness, and people who were scheduled to meet them in later years were not disappointed.

The word "scheduled" may seem a bit mysterious, but it's the right word. Every one of us came into life with a life plan, given to us by Father God so that we can spiritually grow, improve the lives of others, and help Him build a new civilization on Earth. This third part of our life assignment is just as important as the other two because we are helping Father God take back the plan for humanity that has been slowed down by evil but is in no way forgotten about.

Whatever is going on in a person's life, the issues are going to pass if he or she maintains a positive attitude and allows other people to help. There are fantastic helpers who can lead people back to happiness if they will just give the helpers a reasonable chance.

Below are the phone numbers and websites I keep in my billfold at all times so that if I run across someone who I think might be thinking about suicide or knows someone who might be depressed, I can hand them a little three by five sheet, which might save a life. I have this information in a file on my computer so I can easily print out and cut more sheets whenever needed.

National Suicide Prevention Lifeline—1-800-273-TALK (8255)

700 Club: 1-800-759-0700, available at all hours, 24-7

Kenneth Copeland Ministries: 1-817-852-6000

Oral Roberts University Help Line: 1-918-495-7777

HELPGUIDE.ORG: https://www.helpguide.org.

If you know someone you want to help or you are thinking about suicide, please read this Suicide Help article: https://www.helpguide.org/articles/suicide-prevention/are-you-feeling-suicidal.htm.

This is more about the above hotline from the National Suicide Prevention Lifeline website…

We can all help prevent suicide. The Lifeline provides 24/7, free and confidential support for people in distress, prevention and crisis resources for you or your loved ones, and best practices for professionals. Call 1-800-273-8255.

Sometimes all it takes to save a life is to make even a small effort. At my company's website, PathPublishing.com, for many years I have had a suicide prevention article and a link to people to call when a person is depressed; perhaps those links have helped several people over the years. Even if they have helped only one person, that was worth the effort of installing the links and maintaining the website. Every life is precious and unique in Creation.

Recently I have started to make a concerted effort to reach out to people by using the little sheets. I have handed them out to people at two writers' groups; my landlady, who I hope will place them on the table in the front office; and all my friends. Perhaps this can influence the life of someone not too far from me. I can also e-mail the file so that other people can print out sheets whenever they want to, or e-mail it to others. We need to keep trying, if only in small ways, to reach out to those closest to us.

I think the Holy Spirit is in favor of my most recent efforts because I received a vision of a suicide prevention website that I would like to describe to you.

At the top of the front page is the name of the site, which I will let other people decide on. But here is one website description that might work...

A suicide prevention website made by creative people who want to reach out to you.

Then there is an introductory paragraph, something like this...

Welcome to a home for those who are hurting, and possibly contemplating suicide. We are not here to condemn you for your feelings and doubts, but to show you new ways of life, joy, and discovery. Please click on the links below to open yourself to new possibilities and touch base with people who love you, even though they have never met you.

One suicide prevention hotline, open 24-7

One prayer line, open 24-7, with two others that can

assist you if the first line is busy

One link to <u>help lines outside the U.S.</u>

One <u>article</u>

One <u>painting</u>

One <u>video</u>

On <u>sculpture</u>

One <u>song</u>

One <u>poem</u>

One <u>testimonial</u> of a young girl who almost committed suicide and is happy today she did not

One <u>violin concerto</u>

One <u>pastor</u>

One <u>priest</u>

One <u>devotional</u>

One <u>child</u> asking you to choose life

Please don't leave this site if you are still depressed. Call the hotline or one of these prayer lines right now, and give someone a chance to talk with you…

Call 1-800-273-TALK (8255)
700 Club: 1-800-759-0700, 24-7
Kenneth Copeland Ministries: 1-817-852-6000
Oral Roberts University Help Line: 1-918-495-7777

Or read the excellent article at HELPGUIDE.ORG, Trusted guide to mental & emotional health, https://www.helpguide.org; the link is https://www.helpguide.org/articles/suicide-prevention/are-you-feeling-suicidal.htm.

That's the end of the front page of the website.

In Appendix 1 are two creative works which I would allow to be placed at the website for free: a poem called "Night Angel" and a devotional called "Suicide Is a Dead-end."

Appendix 2 contains information that can aid someone outside the U.S. to find help lines to call, taken from HELPGUIDE.ORG, https://www.helpguide.org.

Suicide prevention is close to my heart for many reasons, including the fact that as a teenager I came close to committing suicide. If I had done the horrible act, I would have lost decades of creative work and missed many wonderful people.

I came home from school angry and depressed about something that somebody said. I don't even recall what it was.

Even though I didn't say anything when I walked in the house, my mother noticed there was something wrong with me. When my dad got home from work, she told him that he needed to "Go talk to Johnny."

He found me in the kitchen with a knife. I don't recall his exact words, but he wanted to know what I was doing. I felt like he at least deserved an answer, so I told him what had happened at school. I recall him moving away the knife on the counter, giving me a big hug, and allowing me to cry. He said everything was going to be okay, or words to that effect. I think both of my parents said prayers for me because that negative influence was lifted off me and never came back.

That's my story. I am glad it had a happy resolution.

A couple days after I finished the first draft of this essay I had the following dream, in color, which to me means the dream contains an important message...

I was listening to a well-built fellow from some other country who was aggressively pronouncing the fact that people needed to watch their step when they were around him or he would hurt them. I shook hands with him but his hand was very limp, no strength in it. He went away and I was glad to see he was gone.

In a large room, I was with an acquaintance of mine, who I had some affinity for. He was saying that he still owed money to another fellow, and that the company he works for should not have placed him in that unfavorable position. I could tell he was upset, mentally, emotionally, and even physically. He stepped away to do something else and I was thinking about how I could convince him that forgiveness of all parties was necessary in order to be happy.

Still dreaming, I received an answer to my question about what to tell him. The idea was that when a person is in harmony, it's like energy working within the longitudinal lines of the planet, in order and peace. But when there is unforgiveness, there are swirling energies, like hurricanes, which the positive energy has to go around in order to function. This is a state of disharmony and is an inefficient use of resources.

After I awoke, I did this analysis of the dream: The aggressive man represents people who irritate us. They come on mean and appear to be strong, but they are not, unless we give them power over us. Their strength is eliminated when we hold out a hand of friendship, the hand of love. And they do pass out of our lives if we will allow time for that to happen.

The large room means that there are opportunities for spiritual expansion if we will be aware. My affinity for my acquaintance means that my Spirit and a lot of other people love anyone who is going through trials. His owing money means that he is losing energy, creating a spiritual loss by holding on to negative feelings. His blaming the company for the problem is like all of us when we want to blame circumstances or organizations or God for our trials. His being upset mentally, emotionally, and physically means that unforgiveness causes harm to all parts of a person. And as to the analogy of the planetary energy, for harmony to exist a person has take control of his own world. When he does, when he calls on Jesus Christ to help him, all things are possible. Over time, peace does come.

I leave you with one of my poems...

The Christ Solution

As it is with candle being light
in large room or darkest, lonely night,
so it is with man's trial, that fright
may charge him to succumb.
Yet it is at that moment he might
call out for Christ to come.

(Poetic form: Burns Stanza, a six-line poem
with the rhyme scheme aaabab and
syllable count of 999696)

Chapter 13

The Smaller Words Will Have Their Day,
Just Not Today—Wordy Humor

The meeting was brought to order by With. So it was that The Articles, A, And, and The, met with several members of The Prepositions, most notably With, To, and Into, in order to protest "blatant discrimination when in titles"—that was the exact phrasing in their "Notice Of Assembly."

For as With so eloquently stated, "For too long we Prepositions, and you Articles, have been reduced to lower case status in most publications throughout the English speaking world. While those coordinating conjunctions—Yet, Or, So, But, Nor—for example, have far less length than some of us, yet enjoy capital status."

It was And who interjected at this moment: "My dear With, please note that I, And, am also on occasion considered a coordinating conjunction."

With quickly continued in his same mode of aggression: "That may be true, And, yet you must realize that the rules concerning the decision to elevate you to capital status or reduce you to the lower case are often so confusing that you are, thus, reduced by many writers without thought."

Poor And was made speechless, for With's argument had been directly to the point.

With continued: "It is my concerted belief that we

Articles and Prepositions should unite and boycott all titles unless we are given, as the journalists have done for years, capital status in all headlines."

It was To who raised his hand to speak. "My fellow members of this most industrious gathering, I need to interject that many journalists' organizations have rendered all words in titles, except of course the first word, to lower case status."

With was impatient. "That does not have any bearing on this issue, To. The actions of some journalists to make their jobs easier by ignoring all rules of capitalization do not decrease the mass discrimination in most books, even the rebellious Internet, and those heinous objectors of our quest for capital status, English teachers."

To did not belabor the point, but quietly went into a state of repose.

With paused for a moment, looked deeply into the eyes of several of those who were present, and said: "Are we ready for a vote?"

The motion was seconded by The.

"Then," said With, "we make the resolution whereby all of us, if I may speak for all Articles and Prepositions, now refuse to be used in titles henceforth until we also are capitalized like the 'more important' words!"

There was a resounding "Yea" around the room.

With continued, "Then I count this meeting successfully adjourned."

It was Into who at last made a comment: "Should we not,

for the sake of editors, teachers, and grammarians everywhere, put this pronouncement in writing?"

There was a pause. All motion in the room stopped. It was as if a sudden illumination fell on them, that for all their sustenance as words, none of them knew how to write. And it was And who brought home the realization in verbal form.

They were, as a body, stunned. Without the declaration in writing, their vote could never exist in the real world.

And so, life goes on in the world of words; discrimination in titles continues to abound.

Chapter 14

How the Life Cycle Works for Most People

Much of this chapter is written from the point of view of your Spirit, who you really are at your core. I will do the best I can to make these ideas clear.

1. Typically, before you are born, an angel or a team of angels will...

a. look at your soul, all parts of yourself, to understand what you are in your Spirit being, where you have been, and what kind of life you need to live in order to help you in spiritual and practical understanding.

b. forecast where the world is heading in the next 50 to 100 years, politically, socially, and spiritually. And where you fit in with what the world needs in order to grow spiritually, practically, politically, and harmoniously. For those being born currently, one consideration is the building of the Kingdom of God, our next great civilization.

2. You (as your Spirit) will look around for the right parents needed in order to accomplish the life purpose. Also of importance will be the other members of the family.

Sometimes there is no ideal set of parents. You may have to take second- or third-best (and overcome extra generational curses that really shouldn't be yours) in order to get a body of the right sex and inclinations to do what you need to do. But hopefully you can find a willing couple at about the same spiritual level as yourself.

Not to digress, but sometimes I see this situation in the lives of some people: Once they reach maturity, or even as a teen, they leave home forever. They jump into their true life's work and seldom look back. It's not that they don't love people or appreciate what their parents did for them, but their calling is in a totally different sphere of activity.

Of course, this is not the only reason why some people leave home as soon as possible with a degree of finality. Sometimes childhood was so disagreeable that they don't want anything to do with the past.

3. Once the parents are chosen, you may have to wait a few years for the baby to come along. Sometimes some other soul needs the baby body that is in progress. But you can wait for the right baby body, in most cases. Getting the right parents is very important.

4. You are born. Thank goodness it finally happened. This is important to understand: Sometimes you will take on certain physical handicaps or pass through tough conditions in order to develop one or more character traits, like patience, courage, a forgiving attitude, and so forth. Voluntary trials are not punishment from God. They are your chances to grow inside and improve the world.

Conversely, there are unintended trials. Satan loves to bash us whenever possible. Plus, if parents sinned against the laws in the Bible, children can be affected. You must examine every trial for its true cause. If a bad condition is related to a sin of the parents, like having sex before marriage, they can repent and the physical condition plaguing the child can be totally reversed. I strongly recommend to everyone when they are going through a physical condition to seek out a church that is known for having a healing ministry, where the pastor believes that faith can overcome trials. Healing did not end with the deaths of the apostles.

Let's talk more about miraculous healings for a moment. I am in favor of getting into the Bible and finding key verses that can prepare a person for a radical improvement in their life—be it in the area of healing, prosperity, or deliverance.

I believe that the Early Church preformed miracles because of the powerful presence of the Holy Spirit. We today, as children of God, can do so also. A person should never feel like their life purpose will be jeopardized in any way if they get physically healed of an unwanted condition. There will be plenty of other obstacles in any mortal life after one trial passes into dust!

5. You will go through several years of childhood development in preparation for your life calling. Hopefully these years will not be traumatic and will not interfere with a stable career and marriage. But let's not underestimate the potential in these years to learn life lessons. Every part of life, from childhood to old age, has its lessons to teach.

6. You will begin several decades of active adult life, hopefully gaining spiritually as well as practically and financially. Some people seem to ignore the spiritual side of life, only later, perhaps in old age, realizing the importance of maintaining spiritual considerations.

7. Finally, in the later years there can be a certain satisfaction in all of the successes in business and social life, the children raised, and spiritual blessings that have exceeded expectations.

8. The transition into the next world does not have to be fearful or complicated. It can be a relaxing release of a life that was productive. This is what I wish for all of us.

This has been a short explanation of the cycle of development for most people, but throughout the process there can be an exploration into the work of angels and our own Spirits on subtle planes in order to grow in awareness.

Chapter 15

Finding Life Goals and the Life Mission

Most retired people can look back on their lives and see specific periods, perhaps specific goals they accomplished: childhood's end when adolescence began, first lasting job, marriage and children, with others after those. The point is, a person is much better off if he spends some time early in life finding out what his main life goals are. Then he can make a life plan to accomplish them, releasing objectives that might seem important or more socially acceptable but probably have fewer lasting benefits. Where can he look to find out more about his life goals?

Years ago, a friend of mine and I were discussing life goals. He went away for about an hour and returned with a list of almost a hundred. I suggested that he shorten the list considerably, choosing only one or two for now and letting the rest ride. He said that was impossible. Well, I lost track of my friend eventually, so I don't know how many of his goals have manifested, but of the ones that would take years to get done, probably only two or three. I agree with the idea of writing down desires, hunches, and inclinations—getting it all on paper. I agree with another idea of letting that list stay on the table a few days before making serious decisions. But eventually, a person has to choose a small number of things to work on now, only one big one if possible.

That is not to say that practical and necessary objectives are ignored; they are simply placed in a priority list.

A good look at the past can net clues about life goals. What current obligations need to be met? Maybe some old goals need to be sustained or cleared away before a new one can come in. Paying off a loan on a car or an education might be needed first so that savings can be freed for new adventures.

And what accomplishments in the past can be built on? An interest in music might lead to a pleasant life as a music store proprietor or even a career as a concert musician.

Other sources need to be mentioned. Prayer might be a big help, or daily or weekly times set aside for introspection and pondering about life. Some people have unusual and insightful dreams that, when interpreted properly, can be beneficial. But I have always avoided palm readers or psychics. Astrological forecasting I also avoid.

I guess talking to a counselor or a parent might work, but I have been shy about talking with others about something so crucial. And besides, how are they going to find out what I should be doing? Will they rely on reason or intuition or something else? Will a parent project himself into my life and tell me what he would like me to do when what he says is really something he always wanted to do but was unable?

I can give some hints about what to look for, as far as common goals are concerned. First, all of us need to have a mostly developed physical body by age 12, with mental and spiritual control over that body between 18 and 24. Followed by work on an occupation, marriage, and family for most people. Next come creative years that usually include expansion in work or hobby. Once a life is more or less in order, the 40s are often marked by a greater concern for other families and society in general. At some point down the road, we begin to think about retirement. Following that, we usually prepare ourselves for death in some way.

Dates are not hard-set, and some people leave out or reduce the importance of one or more—no marriage or little social work, as examples. But as a general rule, people develop in a systematic way. Since they do, even a child can have some idea of what personal goals might be coming up.

Usually a life goal is not in direct competition with the goals of other people. If it is, like winning a gold medal at the Olympics, then a person has to assume that his goal may be in jeopardy. For most of us, the completion of a life goal will, in some way, benefit the world and will not greatly conflict with others. In fact, the making of a goal may make someone else's also; if a man and a woman marry, they have both made goals. No one loses.

I need to mention here that once a person begins to seek out life goals, he might discover a goal that was supposed to have been done but was not; at the same time, there is a demanding current goal, and perhaps a third goal looming in the near future. Don't despair! Perhaps the two current goals can be worked on at double the effort and both be done before the next one starts.

All of a person's life goals make up what I call the life mission, which summarizes the whole life and usually can be stated in a single sentence. For example: to use musical talent to entertain people and heighten the vibrations of the world while learning to adjust to situations and people along the way. Another might be to overcome personal handicaps as a child and later aid others through a medical career. The possibilities are limited only by the desires of humans to perfect themselves and simultaneously improve their world.

Chapter 16

Making Life Goals

If finding out life goals is exciting, making them is even more so. One of the great things about living in the West is that people are accustomed to being creative and active, perhaps even too active when they have too much going on at once. But they are doers. The question is, are there some techniques that can assure the accomplishment of a life goal so that everything a person wants to do in a life can get done?

I must begin by saying that a person must believe in the power of mental energy, that mental energy is what makes physical things happen. If strong enough, physical results must happen—eventually, at least. Also, he must assume that directed mental energy is more powerful than undirected energy, or energy that is required to sustain several things. These are pretty basic ideas, but a person has to change into a believer in thought rather than in chance; only then can consistent, positive results occur.

As believing in the power of thought is a must, so is the giving up of things, activities, and even some people that are energy drains. Since I am talking about making a life goal as quickly as possible, it is obvious that every minute spent doing something draining is not forwarding the goal. A number of other things will need to be released, at least for now. Cutting down TV time would hurt very few people. Not playing a game with the guys almost every Saturday, all day long, might be the thing to do. Not visiting a relative with a habitually negative attitude would help. So awareness of time loses and an insistence on priorities is essential. A person might well have a main goal while sustaining a job, a family, and long-term spiritual goals—that's fine. I'm not saying to let go of essentials that need to be maintained.

Now to the goal itself. Let's say I want to start a business in a field I already have some knowledge of; either I have a college degree or I have worked for someone else for a few years. I have given the idea considerable thought for several months and have in my mind a pretty good idea of what I want. I have determined the steps I will need to go through for it to happen successfully.

I will do a careful feasibility study as to the local market's need for my service or product, store location analysis at several spots, supplier availability for what I will need, and so on. I have already worked on getting initial capital and know my banker pretty well. Once my banker gives his okay, I will sign a lease on the building, move in, hire a crew, do the advertising that is appropriate, and have enough cash on hand and in the bank to keep it going until it shows a profit— whereupon I can realize some take-home pay for myself.

How long will this take? Well, not counting my years in college or experience in the field while working for someone else, and the time it took to put away my personal savings that I will have to live on for a while, just thinking it out and knowing exactly what I want will take about half a year, the feasibility study and the banking procedures at least a month, and the moving in and the hiring of a crew about a month. (I'll think about the training of them later.) In another year I should have a profit each month, or at least most months. From start to finish I will need about two years. Without enough personal savings, that might bring complications that add more years to the venture.

The plan has been formed. Each small goal, or sub-goal, like getting the financing or opening the store, can have a deadline. With the sub-goals lined up, the big goal will materialize on time. If I have planned well and don't get too bogged down in details along the way or become discouraged at minor obstacles, I should survive the project with a healthy business that I will enjoy working at for years to come.

Now I start letting positive thinking really work for me. Every thought I have about my business is positive. In my billfold I have placed a piece of paper where I can often read something like: "I am the owner of a successful business." In my self-talk I say that I already have the business, it's doing well, and my employees and customers are happy. In my prayer time, I align my goals with God. Since my subconscious accepts everything I think as real, it accepts the store as real. With my conscious and subconscious minds working hard at this, the manifestation must come.

Each evening I take some quiet time to picture my store. I see myself at my desk going over the day's accounts. I observe the counter where my employees are helping customers and doing great. I live it. I almost breathe it and touch it. I concentrate hard on it and my subconscious goes to work, sending out vibrations that will attract it to me.

Next, I picture each of my sub-goals being accomplished, like flipping through photographs one after another. I finish my prospectus, I get the bank loan, I sign the store lease, I hire employees, I set advertising times, I open the store, I take home my first check. It's real! All of it!

But let us say that in three or four years I do not have my store. What happened? Well, maybe I made a few mistakes along the way or had attitudes that worked against me.

Did I talk to the wrong people? Sure, I had to see my banker, talk to owners of vacant buildings or managers of shopping centers, and contact tax and permit people. But did

I tell the guys at work, relatives in Vermont, and the neighbor's four-year-old? What I needed to do was talk only to necessary people, each one being told only part of the plan that he or she needed to know. Telling other people can hurt me in three ways.

First, this idea of a business is like a seed in a garden; if taken out of my subconscious every few days to show people, I will never grow what I want. Second, they may like the idea and applaud me for my plan. Great, but is that what I want? Applause? If I get too enamored with applause I may settle for that and not the store. And what if they don't like the idea and laugh in my face? How can I keep that strong self-confidence if I open myself up to ridicule or doubt? If I didn't think the idea was sound I wouldn't have seriously considered it in the first place.

But about that original idea. Was it too ambitious? Too idealistic? Maybe the public is not ready for it yet. Did I have all the know-how I needed to accomplish my task? Sure, I didn't expect to know it all, but did I learn as I went? Did I give the idea enough time? Was I too impatient? Was I flexible enough? The idea was pictured in my mind, but did I allow for minor variations in its manifestation? Did I let my idea interfere with past goals that I am now maintaining, which in turn interfered with my current project? Like, did I work 80 hours a week and never see my family? Conversely, did I really work hard enough to make it happen? It's easy to say I did, but a person has to learn to love hard work. Or did I step on other toes while climbing the ladder of success? It's hard enough to succeed without creating animosity; then again, it's also vital to oppose people who try to shut down my right to grow.

Any of these could be the reason for my not having my store. But even in failure (postponed success), did I grow? Did I learn from the experience? Maybe it's just not for me to have right now. Putting it off for a time does not end my desire for it, unless I end my desire for it myself.

Success and failure are two sides of the coin called life. Certainly we can learn, though, how to make the coin come up heads almost every time. Someday every one of us is going to have the ability to make every right idea come up heads. The ability to make life goals leads to successful life missions and to perfection.

Chapter 17

Expanding Time

It's time for us to talk about time. We all deal with time every day in a variety of ways: making our schedules, trying to find time for everything that needs to be done, thinking about what's going to happen next week or next month or next year, remembering the past and what needs to be done to finish things, occasionally considering how short life is, and sometimes remembering friends whose time on Earth has been concluded.

But is time as concrete as we believe? I mean, in our three-dimensional world, we have pretty much controlled, or restricted, our concepts of time. But what if there are more than three dimensions? I don't want to get metaphysical here, but it might give us encouragement if we were to consider time as more far-reaching and more complicated than what we currently hold to be true.

Many science fiction stories and articles have been written about time machines and other futuristic prospects. And some of the technologies and discoveries in science fiction stories have come true. However, in a very real, practical sense, what if God has made plans for us that are more spectacular than what we can currently imagine?

Think back to the founding of the United States. I don't know how much you know about American history and world history, and I'm not claiming to be an expert historian, but from what I have learned from college courses, various readings, and reliable TV programs is that in those days the vast majority of people believed that a country had to have a king in order to survive. They believed that "common people" were simply incapable of making serious government regulations that had wide consequences, within a nation and internationally.

Plus there was a religious connotation attached to kings, that they had a divine right to rule, an anointing from God that they were fully qualified to take the position of king. And no one outside the royal family was qualified.

The historical facts do not always coincide with this, because we can always go back into history, England for example, and read about kings who made a real mess of their time on the throne. But that's another story, or numerous stories with sad endings.

In the early 1700s, and before, there were a few authors who were proposing what we today call representative government, where the people have the authority to elect representatives to make the decisions for them. This was a revolutionary concept, in more ways than one, but gradually, commoners began to believe in this idea.

My point is that God is not isolated off in space somewhere, twiddling His thumbs. He is very active in human life and in human politics. My belief is that He greatly encouraged the political writers with new ideas in order to establish a nation that would be free from kings, free from religious power seekers, and free to allow people to worship as they wish. And it happened. The United States was born.

Since God can see into the future far better than we can, the next idea is that He can see a new nation that is a pure democracy, where we will not need to elect representatives because the people can vote on every new law that is needed.

This will not work in today's societies because there are too many people who cannot rule themselves by the Golden Rule and other basic precepts in the Bible. But my contention is that there is going to be a radical shift in the number of people on this planet. The survivors of that culling will be the people presently living on this planet who, with a bit of training and mind changing, could rule themselves.

The number of laws needed, of course, would be far fewer than what are on the books today. In our next great nation, there might only be one or two dozen new laws every year for the people to consider voting on. This will require the creation of a new, enlightened constitution. But I think these things will come, and not too far into the future.

This future society is so important to me that I have written three books about it. Two are still in print and can be ordered from Path Publishing or Amazon.com. Once again I must refer you to the About the Author and the Publisher section at the back of the book to find out more about *My Visit to the Kingdom of God* and *My Return to the Future, 2350— Our Next Great Civilization Revealed.*

The Bible states that there will be a thousand years in which Jesus rules the nations. "Then I saw the thrones, and those seated on them had been given authority to judge. And I saw the souls of those who had been beheaded for their testimony of Jesus and for the word of God, and those who had not worshiped the beast or its image, and had not received its mark on their foreheads or hands. And they came to life and reigned with Christ for a thousand years" (Revelation 20:4, KJV).

To me, that will take some preparation, most likely another thousand years. Thus we have this time plan:

Jesus comes a few years after the year 2000. This is the

great culling out of humanity. And the reason why so many enlightened people are trying to spread the word to all the world, before hundreds of millions of souls never again have a chance to further spiritually grow on Earth.

Between now and the year 3000, humankind will develop people who are able to rule themselves and gradually organize themselves into our next great civilization. Satan is released in the year 3000, approximately, and is thrown out of the Earth by the combined energy of human beings and angelic forces. Then God can do with Satan as He wishes. God gave human beings the authority to rule Earth and they will take back full authority without great evil interfering.

Between 3000 and 4000 will be the Millennium in which Jesus rules all the Kingdom, all the nations. He will have a physical office in Jerusalem. Any citizen can go there and have an appointment with Him; though, of course, all citizens will have a spiritual relationship with Him.

I hope we can all begin to think of our existence in time as being fluid, like sailing on a boat on an ocean, where we can see farther in all directions than we can on most dirt settings. Let us not limit time or God to our personal, material environments. When we seek His love and appreciation for all of life, our horizons greatly expand.

I wish very much to see you, dear reader, along with all of my friends in the Kingdom. Even if this current physical world and all of its nations pass away, let us not lament. A bright, shining world is straight ahead.

Chapter 18

Faith, Again

Sometimes life throws us some curves, perhaps several curves all at once. And we are not quite sure how to react. This happened to me a few months ago. And in prayer, I turned to God for answers.

Luckily, the things I was going through in life right then were not horrendous. But they were serious, and I was tired of worrying. Since worry is just another version of fear, I didn't want to build fear into my life. This is a lesson I have learned in the last few years.

Rather than words or feelings, I received a vision. I was standing at a precipice. When I went closer, I could see a great canyon. And the problem was, how do I get to the other side? Like the pioneers who crossed the great West, where I live, sometimes they met huge obstacles.

But there was a precipice to get across somehow. Mental reasoning said, "Hire a helicopter. Maybe that would work." But that would be very expensive. So I cried out, "Lord, how do I get across this canyon and over there?"

From behind me, I could see a strong hand dropping a large kite, a device I could crawl into and fly across. I looked it over. I didn't know how to work one of those things. And it was kind of scary, jumping off a cliff and trying to fly something I had never even seen before—daunting, needless to say. But my big question was, "Lord, even if I make it to the side, how do I make sure I get up to the top of the other cliff? I could make it over there and end up at the bottom of the cliff and not be able to climb up."

A peace came over me, as if to say, "Don't worry about it. Once you get over there, the answer will be clear."

So I crawled into the contraption and figured out how to make the parts move. Then the Holy Spirit gave me insights as to how the plastic sheets would work when I was up in the air. So I felt a lot more comfortable about trying it out. I cannot say I was totally confident, but with faith, as it says in the Word, all things are possible.

I walked to the edge of the cliff and waited for the right wind currents to come. I knew I was going to have to wait and get a feel for the wind before making my jump. The wind did rise up, hitting my face. I felt it was not too strong, would not blow me backwards or downwards into the cliff below. So I ran back to the device, quickly got in, ran toward the cliff, and jumped.

I gained control over the big kite and felt exhilarated. I always wondered when I was a boy what it would be like to be a bird—now I was finding out. Big bushes and trees down below looked very small. But my main concern was to keep the machine balanced and me in the air. It wasn't as hard as I expected.

After my jump, I went down for a ways, but the wind caught me, sending me higher than the cliff. But gradually I was descending. I remember thinking, "If I don't get any higher I'm going to crash into the cliff on the other side."

The second most critical moment of my journey was rapidly approaching. No matter what I did to the controls, I didn't go up. The wind was pushing me down, down, down. Should I curve off to one side and land on the valley floor?

But what good would that do me? I'm not a mountain climber. I didn't want to even think about trying to climb the cliff.

I came closer and closer to the cliff side. I said, "Lord, You said to not worry about this. You're going to have to do something!"

But things didn't change. I kept going down toward the bottom of the cliff. Something told me to not give up, not panic, keep going straight ahead. So I did.

Just as I was about to reach the cliff, a point of no return, where there was simply not enough space to turn the craft and head for the valley, I was suddenly whisk up, rapidly, as if God had sent a special breeze, just for me.

Then I thought, "Updrafts! Why didn't I think of that? The updrafts over here will take me up." And they did. I hung on, and up I went. Soon I found myself higher than the cliff ahead of me. I maneuvered the vehicle and came down on the other side, safe and sound.

I said a prayer of thanksgiving. I crawled out of the little craft that had served me so well and looked back across to the cliff I had come from. Then I turned away from that view and started walking on as if nothing happened. End of vision.

I sat peacefully for a few moments, thanking God for taking the time to educate me. It was, once again, my need to rise to new level of faith. I had gone through a number of faith experiences over the decades, but this one was going to be special. Because this time I was going to relax in my faith. I was not going to worry about the ability of faith, and God's power and intelligence, to get me through. I would be using faith again, but not "faith, again, question mark." I would be a mature human being with a mature faith facing issues, this time in peace.

It says in the Word, "If the Son therefore shall make you free, ye shall be free indeed" (John 8:36). And part of that freedom is the freedom from all fear, even when the only thing we have is faith.

Chapter 19

Peace Provision

In a world of chaos, in which there are literally thousands of opportunities to be sad or depressed, especially if one allows time for media contacts, a person needs to build within himself and his home an unmistakable environment of peace.

Some people think, "Once I have done this or that I will have peace." Or, "When I start my vacation I will have some peace." But in reality, peace should not have a beginning or an end point. It should never leave us. As Jesus said, "The thief cometh not, but for to steal, and to kill, and to destroy: I am come that they might have life, and that they might have it more abundantly" (John 10:10, KJV). He did not put a time limit on our peace.

To me, peace starts with a determination to have it and maintain it. And who better to go to find peace than God? On the seventh day of Creation He rested. I don't believe He was tired; I believe He wanted to step back and admire Creation—not in an egotistical sense, but in sheer delight of it all. So too should we delight in our lives. None of us is without flaws or trials, yet none of us is without tremendous achievements, continuous survival through many obstacles, and positive character traits. I think that all the positives add up to the fact that God has not left. He may not be obvious in every moment of every day, but He is present.

So how do we find and maintain more peace? To me, the Bible is a history of God's work on Earth. And more than a history, a roadmap to future discoveries. So by studying the lives of the people in it, and their words of wisdom, peace will naturally come. In a way, peace is like humility, you attain it indirectly. You head in a positive direction and, after weeks or months, you examine yourself and your current situation, finding peace close by.

Then when the next obstacle comes, you can return to your Bible verses and your inner serenity to keep you calm. There may be an initial surprise when the negative situation appears, but you have the Truth of the Word to carry you through.

As discussed elsewhere in this book, the Holy Spirit is very real. Call on Him in times of trial, and anytime you feel stressed out. One technique I have learned to use is this: Like a manager or owner of a company has to learn to delegate tasks to individuals who have been properly trained, when a long-term obstacle comes my way I can say, "Dear Holy Spirit, I delegate that to You." Then I can go about my daily affairs and leave the resolution of that problem to Him. Of course, a person has to build up faith in His abilities to get things done. But I have seen miraculous resolutions, so I know He can get anything done, given enough time. As it says in the Word, "I can do all things through Christ, Who strengthens me" (Philippians 4:13, NKJV).

What is anxiety and how do we control it? Once again I return to the fine dictionary on my computer…

1. feeling of worry: nervousness or agitation, often about something that is going to happen

2. something that worries somebody: a subject or concern that causes worry

To me, anxiety is worry and worry is fear. As the evangelist, Kenneth Copeland, has said: "Fear is faith contaminated." A person is either living in fear or in faith. They do not mix, as oil and water do not mix. A person simply has to decide to rely on faith in God to pull him through; fear, anxiety, and worry must leave.

Here again we have to come back to learning Bible verses and calling out to the Lord for assistance. We cannot allow even minor anxieties to bring us down.

Let's talk about people for a minute. They can be irritating at times, needless to say. But how do we tolerate negative people and the situations they bring to us?

First of all, let's talk about free will. Do human beings have the right to make their own decisions? I'm not talking about one's young children, who must have parental guidance. I am talking only about adults. We have to let other adults make their own decisions. We cannot expect them to be exactly like us. At the same time, we need to, and have the right to, defend ourselves physically or mentally against invasion of our own sovereignty.

Here are some techniques I have learned about dealing with people:

Allow for tolerance. Not everyone is going to agree with everything that we think and we are not going to agree with everything they think or do. That's okay.

We need to forgive everyone of every act they have ever committed against us. This is fully discussed in other chapters in this book.

We need to forgive ourselves of everything we have done

to hurt other people, including sins of omission, like when we did not help others when we could have.

We need to put the other person in the hands of God and let them go. Allow the Holy Spirit to work on their hearts and make them more receptive to God's love and kindness.

Realize that we all have different talents, and we are all on various levels of development within the wide range of character traits. As a schoolchild may be slow in developing math skills, he may be very good at sports and so-so in reading development. So too, a person might be courageous, yet impatient about many things, and at least mildly tolerant—all at the same time.

Use avoidance whenever possible. For a schoolchild, if you know a bully hangs out on a certain corner, walk home a different way. For an adult working in an office, if you know a fellow worker has a touchy area, don't bring it up in conversations. If your spouse has a trouble spot, pray about the resolution of that issue. When you are planning out your life long-term and you feel like you would be better off by not marrying anyone, that you have a lot of things to do in life, don't marry. Don't have sex outside marriage and don't feel guilty about never getting married.

Use patience with people. It's hard to change any habit, and for a habit or attitude to change, a person really has to want to make it happen. Same with people reacting to you: They are never going to change until there is a real need to change, until they have a revelation that the current way of acting or thinking needs to be improved. It may, or may not be, your responsibility to let them know that one of their attitudes needs work. But you can always pray for them.

Peace is always within you. Since peace is part of God, and God dwells in you, there is at all times a part of you that stays in peace, no matter what happens. Your task is to align yourself with that part, and never depart.

Chapter 20

Boring Names—More Wordy Humor

Years ago, I was watching a TV show about a town in Oregon named Boring. I don't recall much about the show because, quite honestly, it wasn't real exciting. The highlight of the program was a conversation with a man named Boring who owned a big business in Boring, which, not surprisingly, had been named after one of his Boring relatives—maybe a grandfather. I may have some (or most) of these facts wrong. I don't know. I didn't take notes.

Not all of the facets of the family's history were revealed in the TV show. Not everything is fit for TV. But everything (just about) is fit for print, so here goes.

As I was surfing the Internet one day, I stumbled onto these facts, which are not boring, though not exactly mind teasers, either. Well, anyway...

The man who I believe the film crew interviewed was Ira Ben Boring, I.B. Boring for short. I found out that at an early age he fell in love with a girl in his hometown, Ursula Beth Smitherton. That would make her, once married, U.R. Boring.

They had two daughters, who they named Ima Boring and May Bea Boring. They got a little tired of the ribs they were taking after the editor of the local newspaper, Max Plank, was playing around one day, reduced the parents' names to initials, and wrote an article about them in *The Boring Times*.

Ira and Ursula named their next child Thomás Lee Boring—with the accent on the *mas* (in order to appear "uppity"?) so their Boring initials would be dismissed from their neighbors' minds ASAP. About a year later, after Thomás began to talk, he could not pronounce his given name; all that came out of his mouth was Toto. (Like the dog in *The Wonderful Wizard of Oz*—maybe that's where he got the sounds, watching the movie.) So Toto, stuck. On the boy's first day at kindergarten, he was Toto Lee Boring.

I can't back up this article by showing confirming research from my local library, and I know it all seems far-fetched, so you can believe it if you want to. Yet, stranger names have been applied at times to members of the human community. Like, have you read the family history of the grocery store magnate, H.E. Butt?

Chapter 21

The Price of Fame

Someone asked me once to name something that is not physical yet society says is highly valuable and many people seek, and may contain serious flaws. The answer to the riddle was *fame*.

What is fame? When I return again to the dictionary on my computer I find this primary definition with a side note which I have paraphrased...

Renown: the condition of being very well known; the fame that goes with being a recording star, for example.

The word fame comes from 12th century words that mean "talk, report, reputation."

Let me say up front that I have no complaint about someone being well-known for a lifetime of good service. Those people exist in every community in our nation, though we still don't consider them famous. We think of famous as being someone on TV or in the movies. And that is the subject of my discussion.

Millions of people have given up their hometown life, which could have been filled with a job, family, and church, in order to get in a car, drive to Hollywood, and try to "make it big." It's not that I am against Hollywood in its entirety; it's that dreams are usually shattered in its environments. Not only do most people never achieve the fame that they desire when they go there, many years, perhaps decades, are lost in the struggle. Yet, oddly enough, some of the greatest tragedies happen when they do achieve a degree of fame, or at least some success in the entertainment industry.

One of my objections to this mode of thinking is that it's all surface stuff. We start with a pretty or handsome face (without this, a person is relegated to becoming a character actor, very seldom having the lead in a motion picture). Have you ever noticed that most of the "bad guys" and wayward women in motion pictures are still relatively good looking? It's like a person has to be attractive even if playing the part of an unattractive person.

The second flaw is that, in order to succeed in Hollywood a person has to adopt a kind of power worship, where the people in control, or "in the know," are sought after for their ability to get parts for people and jobs for producers, directors, and technical crews. I understand the need for networking within any industry, but there seems to be little concern about the lack of integrity of some of those being sought out.

Third, there are temptations every step of the way. If one is to get a part, is it okay to stab somebody else in the back, so to speak? Is it okay for a woman to go to bed with a married producer in order to get an acting part? Is it okay for a producer to take money under the table in order to give parts and jobs to people? Is it okay to have a homosexual relationship with someone in order to advance within the ranks? Is it okay to attend parties where women wear dresses that are "showy" and hard drugs and liquor freely flow, perhaps leading to serious addictions and ruined lives? And the list goes on.

I don't deny the fact that occasionally Hollywood comes

up with a truly inspirational and helpful movie. But most of the time, their productions are violent and promiscuous. Early on in my career as a writer, I examined the Hollywood formula. Basically, it's a long series of negative events, mixed in with sexual overtones or worse, with destruction of physical objects playing a vital part in creating sensations. If nothing is destroyed or criticized or at least threatened, it doesn't get in the script. Personally, I get tired of scene after scene after scene in which someone is molested, verbally cut down, or endures suffering in innumerable ways.

Whatever happened to the movies of the 1940's, where boy meets girl, boy and girl fall in love with each other, barriers appear that limit their chances of getting together, he continues trying to make things go well financially and in every other way, there is comic relief along the way, and eventually they get together as a married couple? End of story. The audience leaves the building entertained, while nobody got seriously hurt.

Nowadays, the movies of the 1940s are considered much too tame. The movie magnets tell us that audiences would not attend movies without events that reveal serious conflict. But what has this perpetual blasting of the human consciousness done to most people who partake of mainstream entertainment?

According to one protection group, who is not located in California, the United States has 5% of the world's population yet houses 25% of its prisoners. Why is that? Why do millions of men and women spend perhaps half of their lifetimes (if they are not executed) behind bars? Have we ever thought to look at their childhood and adolescent years to see how much TV they watched?

Well, another authority did just that. Their conclusion was that Saturday morning cartoons are even more violent than weekday evening adult dramas. More characters are killed, force is used in a variety of ways, and the hero's goal usually is to get somewhere before somebody else does or get something somebody else has. And even if the "good guy" accomplishes what he wants, he seldom does so by compassion, understanding, patience, or love.

So our children, young ones and teens, are continually bombarded, week after week, by heroes with less and less compassion. When they grow up and become the people who control our nation, are we to expect them to be like Mr. Lincoln or Mr. Jefferson? How could that ever happen?

I'm not bashing younger generations. Any flaws in their minds are not totally their fault. It is the responsibility of adults to clean up entertainment streams, not the young people who have to endure them. However, it is the responsibility of young people everywhere to reject the money-based programming that they are subject to. It's better to read or listen to a classic from the library and be less aware of what one's peers are hailing as the latest sensation.

Nowadays, once our young ones become adults, they "advance" into adult TV programs. It is my contention that crime dramas lead young people into lives of crime, not away from criminal acts. Just because the "good guy" or police officer nailed the criminal and got him or her put behind bars, does not mean that viewers learn nothing about the life of crime. A person who wants to be a criminal, perhaps feeling like society offers him nothing in the way of a good job, can be trained as a criminal almost every night by watching TV. He does not have to find a college, perhaps get in serious financial debt, study and work hard, try to graduate with honors, search for a job, spend years paying back college loans, and eventually have enough to get by on, debt free.

No, he can recall the thousands of TV shows he has

watched, pick up tricks there, find someone already in the criminal world, watch more TV shows for additional training, and then start stealing as best he can.

True, in five or ten years the police have put him behind bars—similar to the ones he saw on TV. But few criminals have five-year or ten-year plans of advancement. They are more concerned about paying this month's rent at any cost.

For viewers of all ages, how do TV crime dramas and movies affect our subconscious minds? How much chaos and stress do they create while they usually at the same time lead us away from wholesome values that are relaxing?

Everything the subconscious mind views on the big screen is considered real. The cells in our body do not have the mental capacity to say, "This is just a made up story and is make believe." No, they live it as reality, just as real as anything you do outside the theater. When you watch a violent movie, you are in a sense saying that this is what you want your subconscious mind to recreate in every aspect of your life, not just your entertainment hours.

On the positive side, I applaud Christian networks and PBS, to a degree, for year after year giving our young people positive experiences. I do not find all of the so-called Christian movies to be truly Christian. Some of them are no more Christian than secular dramas, in which a tremendous amount of evil is done; only in the "Christian movie" there are five minutes at the end where the villain repents and comes to know a spiritual future. This is no more authentic than if a person put white icing on a chocolate chip cake and called it angel food.

I'm not saying that everything in Hollywood is bad. I'm not saying everything on TV is bad for us. But I do think every individual has to carefully examine their entertainment preferences. Our future lives are determined by our thinking and our emotions, and they cannot be uplifting, positive, and stable if our minds are bombarded every day by influences that are just the opposite.

Chapter 22

Our Next Great Civilization

When I thought about writing an essay for this book concerning our next great civilization, which I have already written books about, I was blessed with a vision of Jesus.

He didn't say anything, just pointed to a hill not far away. Which I went to, by thought in a spiritual body, and saw again the great city, with its marvelous round buildings downtown, quiet factories, and homes spreading in all directions.

Why do I keep returning to this subject over the decades of my life? Why do you return home each day after work or school? Because it is your home. And this fantastic collection of city-states will be our home for several thousand years. I could say, beyond Earth, because living in this Kingdom will change us into beings who will live forever, even in a conscious and physical sense if desired, and last long after Earth is no longer our home. For a much fuller description of the Kingdom, or Kingdom of God, I will leave you to read the two books already mentioned.

But I want this short article to be an introduction to the Kingdom for readers who have perhaps never even thought about it.

First of all, we do not have to be Biblical scholars in order to realize that we are in the times described in the last book of the Bible, Revelation. We simply have to realize that there will be trials ahead and there will be a trimming out of individuals who do not love God and their fellow humans enough to qualify themselves for potential citizenship in the Kingdom of God. Being removed from further life on Earth is not punishment from God, but a welcomed release for most of humanity.

Whether you believe in a pre-tribulation rapture or a post-tribulation rapture we are going to eventually enjoy much brighter days. Eventually there will be only good people on Earth and those living in Heaven will be our spiritual partners.

As it says in the Word, this new influx of strong love will "...cast the unprofitable servant into outer darkness—there shall be weeping and gnashing of teeth" (Matthew 25:30). The Antichrist and his followers, especially the Beast, who carries out his plans, will all be destroyed.

About the same time, all or most of the evil spirits working for Satan are also cast out. Satan and perhaps a few of his followers will withdraw to the center of the planet and stay there, being a much reduced foe to human progress from that time forward.

The positive people here on Earth will find themselves totally free to pursue whatever they wish, free from spiritual hindrances that have been a burden for thousands of years— social and political generational curses, in a sense. It is like a great dawn will appear in human history, enabling people to dream higher dreams than they ever have before.

The space between Heaven and earth will seem to be much reduced. There will more communication than ever before, a flow of energy between these two. In other parts of this book I have mentioned the reality of angels; and in the Kingdom of God angels will be as close as our next-door neighbors.

Throughout His ministry, Jesus was talking about a very real civilization when He discussed the Kingdom. That's why the authorities, both Roman and Jewish, were so concerned about His preaching. They, of course, thought He was talking about raising an army. No, He was talking about the times in which we live today.

Jesus also said that the Kingdom was like a man who found treasure on a piece of land and gave up everything he owned so he could purchase it. "Again, the kingdom of heaven is like unto treasure hid in a field; which when a man hath found, he hideth, and for joy thereof goeth and selleth all that he hath, and buyeth that field" (Matthew 13:44 KJV). On the surface, if a man sells everything he owns in order to purchase barren land, he may look foolish to his neighbors. But after he digs up his treasure, he will be well off. Christians look foolish to the world: Christians are always looking for something beyond, not so concerned with material blessings or fame, generous beyond common sense, and forgiving and loving toward people who otherwise might not ever be loved. But to those of us who follow Christ, the rewards in the future will be far beyond the expectations of those in the secular world.

With all the evil passed away, the plans and energy for the Kingdom of God will fully manifest. "And I saw the Kingdom of God descend from Heaven. And Jesus carried me away in the spirit to a great and high mountain, and shewed me that great city, the holy Jerusalem, descending out of heaven from God" (Revelation 21:10).

To give you just a few hints about how wonderful our future can be, here is a segment near the end of *My Return to the Future, 2350*, which has fictional elements in order to make it more entertaining to most readers. In the story, the family members who I meet in the New World go to a concert one night under the stars. Lying on the grass near Sandreen, the mother, and the others, I listen to a fantastic orchestra. I have these experiences…

I relaxed. I felt all the tension leave my body. It was like I was also letting go any residual tension from my former life. I felt a supreme joy from hearing the music and being around those people. I felt camaraderie with the whole Kingdom, the love of Heaven descending and surrounding us all. Like the first few moments when I arrived in the New World, sitting on the grass near their house, I once again felt that peace that was so characteristic of this place and so very distant from my former life. Here there was *no threat* to my existence. I didn't have to worry about any of these people physically hurting anybody else. I didn't have any demons attacking my mind or brain. It was almost like the priorities of my very being had been placed in order: I was, above all, a Spirit, and my mind, emotions, and physical body were tranquil levels of energy that God had given me to peacefully dwell inside of. There was no rush to do or say anything. So I enjoyed life, energy, true substance, without any demands whatsoever.

In this quiet state I heard one of my favorite pieces of all time, one of Bach's hymns. The peace within that music took me to an even higher state. In my Spirit I traveled far above that physical setting, quite literally into one of the higher planes of Heaven. I looked about me. I intuitively knew that this heavenly state had been united with physical existence below. And I understood that as humankind continued to grow, there would be little separation between the two worlds for most people.

As the distinction between 21st century time and 24th century time had been blurred, so now was the distinction between Earth and Heaven. For me, there was a keen sense that I was now living more in the fourth dimension than I ever had before. It was difficult to explain, even to myself. So

I didn't try. As Sandreen had said, describing the third dimension to an animal is hard. So there I was, without barriers to a greater awareness, letting the experience fill me. I did not attempt to take anything from it.

What I saw was a long line of dimensions, perhaps as many as 50, and I possessed about a fifth of them, if I counted seven dimensions of atomic consciousness in my body. I could see that if I were patient, and always fell within God's wishes, every one of those dimensions would at some point be mine. But there was absolutely no rush for me to attend to anything in regard to attaining them. Everything in the universe, all life, all time, all space, was already possessed and known within God. And by aligning myself, as limited as I might be as a human being, with God, Who already is and possesses all, and is continually giving life and love, I could reach a new step for me, a new awareness. No matter how many beings had come before me or would come after me, my step into this new, fourth dimension, would be new for me, and very precious.

Not only would my step into this greater awareness of life help me, but also enliven the progress of every being on the planet.

That was a startling concept, how I was not only connected to every other living thing, but that everything would be improved when I was improved.

This also made me more aware of my moral responsibilities, even in regard to every individual thought. I should be very careful in every thought I created because every thought had an influence on life itself.

Beyond that, I very clearly beheld the three-dimensional love of God, felt the life energy that He supplies me with every day in order to have a human existence. Simultaneously,

I somehow understood that He was now going to increase that energy so I could do more good.

He was going to allow me to never again physically die.

He was going to allow me to move myself anywhere on this planet that I wanted to go to by thinking myself there. And if I wanted to, I could travel beyond this planet, within reason. The bounds of that travel would be known later.

He was going to allow me to see everything in my long past and my distant future, according to probabilities now in existence.

He was going to show me every aspect of myself. I thought I already knew a great deal about that, but there was more to learn. For example, He was going to improve my character. I believed that the time would come when I simply could not say anything unkind. Perhaps not even think anything unkind.

I could look at a pathetic human being, who had made tons of mistakes, who thought himself unworthy of any love or grace, and say to him, "I offer you a new life. In the Name of Jesus Christ, I pronounce you a new person if you will but believe on Him."

And I could further say to that little human being, "I was once like you. I was lost. I hurt others and I was hurt. And sometimes I wanted to hurt them because they had hurt me. But once I realized that it was a cycle of energy that I had to break, with the help of Jesus, I did turn the other cheek. I let them hurt me and I did *not* retaliate. Other humans thought I was a fool, but I freed my soul from that vicious cycle of pain."

And then, I could reach out with my arms and enfold that

little human being and shed tears that would fall on his neck. And he would hug me. And he would also cry.

I saw that experience multiplied a thousand times. Every day I or someone like me would reach out their arms to a hurting human being. That would be my new life. I would have to give up human existence, with all of its joys and sorrows, in order to visit hurting human beings.

And I said, "Yes, that is the new life I want."

I returned to my physical body lying there on the grass. I opened my eyes and saw at one time, not a thousand stars, but a thousand tears. And they were all washed away, as it says in the Bible.

All of my tears, past and present, in that same moment were washed away—for a man, or a Spirit, must receive grace when he does well for the least of these.

In conclusion, I just want to say that our future is totally optimistic. When I had my first dreams and visions about the Kingdom, back in the 1970s, they changed my opinions about the future, leading me to a great deal more optimism than what most people can accept.

Our future really is very bright despite the trials ahead. I mean, has there been any generation since the fall of Adam and Eve that has not had trials? Is there any place in the world where people have no spiritual or social issues? And isn't it worth it to go through this life in order to get to a Kingdom which will lead us to an eternal life?

I leave you with peace, the peace that you truly are. Go within yourself, find that peaceful place in you, your personal Kingdom of God, which is the starting place for your being a citizen in the Kingdom of God.

Chapter 23

Perfect Patience

Recently I was listening to a pastor making light of his efforts to learn patience. He said that years ago he prayed, "Lord, I need to learn patience, so hurry up and give it to me." He continued by saying, "Later on, I asked the Lord to help me learn patience, but if I'd known what I was going to have to go through, I would never have asked."

I think we can all learn more patience. But, like humility, we can only learn it by doing rightly, and then letting the positive character trait develop on its own. It's as if we cannot go at these two virtues directly. They come as a result of long, positive effort. But, they do come.

By patience, I don't mean that we passively wait on conditions to get better and call that patience. I think whenever anything needs to be done, even if it is a long-term project, we need to work at it at every opportunity.

I am reminded of the phrase in the Bible about waiting on the Lord. "But they that wait upon the LORD shall renew their strength; they shall mount up with wings as eagles; they shall run, and not be weary; and they shall walk, and not faint" (Isaiah 40:31, KJV).

To me, patience means doing whatever you can while waiting on the Holy Spirit to take action with you, to be your partner in whatever you are doing.

In a sense, patience is the ability to forestall action when the time is not right. For years, as a teenager, I played chess with my friends at least once a week. One thing I learned was, you may have an idea for a move, but you might have to prepare for it. You may have to make two or three moves in order to spring the winning move on your opposition. If you make the move right now, you would be in big trouble. So you do what you can to prepare for it.

Sometimes in chess, games are won by positional play. That is, a skilled player can build up tiny positive developmental moves that each in itself would not be dominant, but in combination they overwhelm the opposition. These gradual positional developments are sometimes subtle, but they are based on good chess logic.

Same in life. We don't always win our big successes by going at them with a huge amount of energy this month or this year. We might develop a career game plan like this one: graduate from high school, spend our first two years in a junior college and decide on a major, finish off the last two years at a university, find an entry level position in a good company that is stable, be an excellent employee, take additional responsibilities, and reap monetary benefits that we could never achieve in a single year of effort.

A terribly impatient person may be always looking for get-rich-quick schemes. He may find one or two that prove lucrative, but then he might also invest his money in the next scheme and lose everything. As far as his relationships go, he might leave a long trail of individuals who have ill feelings toward him because they were exploited or their feelings were ignored. So by his impatience, he is at some point going to have to completely start over. That will mean years lost, in contrast to the person who had reasonable objectives both in career and character development.

So in a sense, you could say that patience pays great

dividends. The world, especially in entertainment and media circles, is enamored by the youthful success idol. And they will send him or her to the forefront of their attention even if the person has a great need of character development. Often, what the world calls success is really not beneficial or kind to the one who is given what is perhaps undeserved fame. The individual is being used as a marketing tool by many people, and he will be quickly replaced by the next idol. The brother of Elvis Presley said that the prescription drugs did not kill Elvis before he could ever arrive at old age; what killed him was the loss of fame.

When we look back at all the individuals or entertainment groups who have been placed high on the ranks of success, where are they in five or ten years? The ones who are still around may not be at the tops of the charts, shall we say, but they continue to do the work they love and they show patience.

That reminds me of something a friend of mine told me recently. Her granddaughter came up to her and said, "Mimi, did you know that Paul McCartney had a band before Wings?"

I have never met Paul McCartney, but I have heard that he has tremendous humility. I have talked to Jim Wilson, the extraordinary piano player and composer, who once was hired by Paul McCartney to tune his piano. Paul treated him like an old buddy, with humility, humor, and good taste. Paul McCartney is the kind of guy you could live your life with and never, over the years, have a single regret. Unfortunately, you cannot say that about all musicians. But Paul is having a great deal of fun doing creative things that will long outlive his body.

In short, let's work at patience patiently, by letting it come to us. We might wake up one day and discover that we are much more patient with our spouse or children than we used to be. Even if that realization does not come until we are much older, isn't it worth waiting for?

Chapter 24

Time to Seriously Think about Time

I think in the next few hundred years there will be a revolution in how we think about time. Not just in how we live our lives, but how we live our eternal lives.

Most people believe that they are physical bodies and a Spirit, if there is such a thing, is going along for the ride, is attached to some obscure place on the person and is to be, at best, relegated to Sunday morning thought. This leads to lives of relative insignificance and a slavish conformity to externals.

But what if time is mostly a mental concept that we use to connect physical actions? While the true relationship of all events lies within a Spirit being who is the primary controlling entity over every aspect of the personality and has connections with God, Who is the controlling agent over everything that exists within the universe?

When we consider our personal Spirit as being real—who is in reality our best friend, who is in reality a source of creativity and not boredom—we develop individually and become an instrument to advance humanity more rapidly.

One thing that my Spirit has impressed upon me over the years is that if I forget to work with him, that's very selfish. I may have ideas and desires to serve humanity, but he counts too. Anything incompatible with his wishes should not be pursued. In the long run, I have found that listening to him is a great time saver.

That brings me to another point. Humanity, as a whole, doesn't know where we are going or why. The normal consensus is that a person needs to go after material accumulation because there isn't much else of interest. Even for spiritual people the main concern is about getting to Heaven, where everything will be taken care of—beyond that, there isn't much else to do. The Kingdom of God that Jesus spoke about is relegated to, at best, a consciousness within a human being, with connections to other human beings and God.

But what if the Kingdom of God is going to be a very real civilization on Earth where an examination of time is going to lead us to a revolution in consciousness? What if we can expand time in so many directions at once that it circles back to us, our spiritual selves, and brings with it an understanding of the unity of all time and space?

I don't mean to get too metaphysical here, but I need to say that we need to take the limits off time itself. Why should we continue to limit ourselves to being physical personalities on a planet 93 million miles from one of the many suns in our universe? What if we did a mind shift and looked at ourselves as beings within the universe who can look back at our planet and physical life as a temporary situation? What if we can relax into the enormous complexity within tremendous diversity, in a spiritual sense?

When our scientists consider traveling to Mars, they get out their mathematical pencils and high-tech computers and start drawing trajectories through outer space. I'm not saying this is wrong, but the whole premise is that we need to place a physical body in a physical spacecraft and hurl it to another physical planet. And in this way we will find out more about ourselves. But what if we started to find out more about ourselves by sitting in our own rooms and projecting ourselves in a wide variety of ways? Why must space exploration ignore the spaces in us?

At some point, let's answer this question: Who is God and what is He up to? Most Christians believe that God is our good Father and He loves us. And His desires are mostly to get us through a physical existence and into the peace of Heaven. Those are good wishes. But what if He also has long-term goals for us? What if we are to be radically remade into spirit-beings who have no more limitations in the physical world than a bird has in the world of snakes? We need to have a total mind shift, turn the coin completely over, shall we say.

If we look at an old U.S. quarter, we can see the face of George Washington. If we turn the coin over, we see an eagle, with wings spread. That does not mean that the human face on the other side has been totally erased. It just means we can't see it. Turning the coin back over, we once again see George, and that doesn't mean that the eagle on the back has been erased. So too with our spiritual selves. Why must we only look at one side of life, the physical, and ignore a much wider experience of energy which could enable us to soar far beyond current physical expectations and limits?

Some people are afraid to look at the other side of their own life, the spiritual side. They are afraid that if they look at it, it will somehow interfere with their primary image. When in reality, they will never experience their true potential until they allow both sides to live mutually in respect.

What if we, for example, are to have on a daily basis, the mobility, high character development, and desire for service that characterize angels? Why can't this be our goal instead of simply going into a peaceful state that doesn't have much beyond it? As for me, give me angelic life and leave the physical world behind.

Some people might say that becoming an angel-like being would take too much time, that since we can't make that goal within the limits of our physical lives currently, it's absurd. My comment is that we are eternal, spiritual beings, passing through relatively short physical lifetimes, and we should not limit ourselves in any way. If God, in His Word, does not set tremendous limits on us, then why should we? The Bible says, "I can do all things through Christ, Who strengthens me" (Philippians 4:13 NKJV). It does not say: I can do all things through Christ Who strengthens me in physical life, and not anywhere beyond. So I am all for the pursuit of angelic life as the goal of human life. And even higher dimensions beyond those enjoyed by angels. Why limit ourselves at all?

I know I posed many questions in this essay, perhaps more questions than answers. But we need to get out of our box-like limitations, where nothing matters more than survival and relief from human conflicts. These too will pass. So where do we want to pass to? I vote for infinity.

Appendix 1

Suicide Prevention Poem and Devotional

Night Angel

"It's not worth it." In the dim light of the room
behind the cafe, the blond-haired boy cried.
And she listened, the vision in space that loomed
above dirty floor and faded T-shirt beside
the gun he did not use that night because
the inch of love she gave him kept him from it.
He was married with four children when he paused
long enough on his short couch to again sit
with old times, and the one night that would have
ended it. He did not pray often, but he
said a thank-you to the Powers That Be, glad
his children had a father who loved them. She
heard his prayer, though far away, above
one of his children, thanking God for fatherly love.

Suicide Is a Dead-end

"I shall not die, but live, and declare the works of the
LORD" Psalm 118:17 (KJV).

Everything in life can atoned for—except suicide. If you
crash your car, make a big financial mistake, or lose the
spouse you dearly love, you can buy another car, start a new
business, or date somebody else in a few months or years.

Suicide is a dead-end you don't come out of. You can't say, "OOPS, mistake, sorry." Nobody can help you regain your physical body.

If you need a vacation from life, take it. Take a long trip in your car or on a boat and meet new people. Maybe all you need is a vacation.

I heard this story once: A teenager met a very special girl who he wanted as his wife and raise children with. But she killed herself—to punish her alcoholic father. The young man was, of course, devastated. Later in life he married someone else, but he always felt his life had been altered, was not the beautiful experience it could have been with his first love.

I think most people intellectually understand that they are spiritual beings and suicide is a false idea. The lucky people dismiss it quickly. Others have to work at letting it go. Either way, it needs to be dismissed as illogical, sad, *solving nothing.*

A person needs to understand that love is more powerful than any idea. Our love, together, can overcome anything, and has done so many times.

Dear God, we pray that all Your children fully understand that You accept the fact that they will fail at times to live up to expectations. But at those times, they need not kill themselves, but rely on Your mercy to take them back.

Appendix 2

Finding Suicide Prevention Help Lines Outside the U.S.

This is information taken from HELPGUIDE.ORG, https://www.helpguide.org...

To find a suicide help line outside the U.S., visit IASP or Suicide.org.

About the Author and the Publisher

About the Author

John Schmidt has published almost two dozen works, through his publishing company, six other publishers, and ebook publishers. For more than two decades he has been the editor of Path Publishing, releasing the works of more than 20 authors. In addition, he has earned Master's Degrees in English and in Drama; spent several years teaching college English as an adjunct professor and high school English; penned more than 4,000 poems; developed skills for writing in several genres, from nonfiction books to plays to poems to short stories; and has always encompassed a great love for creative expression and the human experience. He lives in Amarillo, Texas, and is the Membership Coordinator for the Hi-Plains Poetry Society and Inspirational Writers Alive!, Amarillo Chapter.

Connect with John Schmidt:

By e-mail: Path@PathPublishing.com

Check out PathPublishing.com for more information about his books. On menu bar, click on "Most of the Books by John Schmidt."

Amazon.com Author Page:
https://authorcentral.amazon.com/gp/books/book-detail-page?ie=UTF8&bookASIN=1500531316&index=default

Facebook John Schmidt:
www.facebook.com/john.schmidt.716195

Facebook Path Publishing:
www.facebook.com/pages/Path-
Publishing/110081005733297?sk=notes

Final words from John: "Many thanks to my readers! Please remember to leave a review for my book at your favorite retailer."

About Path Publishing

Path Publishing began in 1993 and has published a variety of uplifting books and other projects over the years. The company tends to specialize in Christian nonfiction, poetry, biographies, and self-help. The website, PathPublishing.com, contains the works of numerous writers. In the past, the company has been in these publications: *Christian Writers' Market Guide*, *The Directory of Little Magazines and Small Presses*, and *The Writer*.

Books and Ebooks by John Schmidt

The cost of a paperback copy of *Making Life Work for You* is $7.99. Purchase from Amazon.com or by mail. Postage is $3.50 for the first item and 75 cents for each additional. With the shipping, the cost of one book is $11.49. Texas residents need to add 8.25% sales tax, which comes to $12.44. Send bank check to Path Publishing, 4302 SW 51st Ave. #121, Amarillo, Texas 79109-6159. For inquiries, e-mail Path@PathPublishing.com. Thank you!

To order a copy of either of the other two books mentioned within this volume, the same purchasing opportunities apply. *My Return to the Future, 2350* is only $9.99 and *My Visit to the Kingdom of God* is $13.99.

To find out about John's other works, read the list below or go to PathPublishing.com. On menu bar, click on "Most of the Books by John Schmidt."

Other paperbacks for adults by John Schmidt:

Discover more about yourself within the lives of others, while enjoying a variety of poetic forms, by reading *A Life to Share—Two Hundred Poems for Living Life to the Fullest.* Only $6.99 at Amazon.com, 132 pages.

About 90 of John's poems are in *Winner's Wisdom—Eight-Week Devotional Using Poetry and Journaling to Express the Real You.* Available at Amazon.com for $8.99, 144 pages.

Almost all of his art poems are in *Rock Solid Concrete Poems—Art Poems for the Heart.* You can purchase the paperback at Amazon.com for $7.99. Here are short comments from a reviewer and three readers... "Poetry flows into shapes that pop off the page!" "Texas poet John Schmidt is a master at writing shaped verse/concrete poetry." "Well-crafted, humorous, and pleasurable—a sheer joy to ponder and to read aloud." "The poems are beautiful, not only in words but in design."

If you are looking for a novel, please consider *Timeless Sisters—A Novella About Love in All of Its Dimensions*, where two very different, motherless sisters seek the loves of their lives while dealing with a turbulent time in their country's history when their father, the king, dies suddenly. Paperback is $5.99 at Amazon.com and the ebook is available from Smashwords.com for only $2.99.

Forty Tips for Church Growth—A how-to guide for practical expansion, $4.99. Also an ebook for the same price at Smashwords.com.

Friends Forever, You and God—A Coloring Book for Adults and Children, $5.50.

Smashwords.com ebooks by John Schmidt:

Timeless Sisters, $2.99.

Forty Tips for Church Growth—A how-to guide for practical expansion, $4.99.

Backlist—the following works by John Schmidt can be ordered by mail only (for information, e-mail PathPublishing.com)...

Giving to Yourself and Letting Happiness Happen, $6.99. A great little book for anyone who is seeking a way out of depression.

Our Dream Language, $5.95. A handbook for the dream interpreter, who will discover that the language of dreams is as understandable as any foreign language, with persistence and a reliance on intuitive understanding.

Audio book:

Silly Willy Will, a two-cassette collection of John's poetry, $6.00.

Fiction paperbacks for youths:

The Lion Princess—Journey to an Awakening, $12.95.

Heroes, Angels and Miracles—Eleven Uplifting Stories from Around the World for Youths, $25.00, 360 pages. "Timeless Sisters" is one of the stories in this book.

Children's books:
Purchase all three for only $10.00.

Mr. Turtle's Award, $6.00.

You and God Together, Friends Forever, $6.00.

Two Stories for Children—Betty Blooper Is Super! and Hands Holding Heaven, bilingual, English and Spanish, $6.00.

www.ingramcontent.com/pod-product-compliance
Lightning Source LLC
Chambersburg PA
CBHW061735020426
42331CB00006B/1246